My Story Remembered

R. LaMon Brown
aka PapaMon

Parson's Porch Books

My Story Remembered
ISBN: Softcover 978-1-951472-79-5
Copyright © 2020 by LaMon Brown

All rights reserved. No part of this book may be reproduced or transmitted in any form or by any means, electronic or mechanical, including photocopying, recording, or by any information storage and retrieval system, without permission in writing from the publisher.

www.parsonsporch.com

My Story Remembered

Contents

Introduction 7
The Beginnings of My Religious Life 12
High School Years 14
Beginning My Life with Pat 16
My Religious Life in High School and Early College 17
College Years 20
and Early Married Life 20
Beulah Baptist Church, Albertville, and the Charismatic Movement 27
New Orleans and Tangipahoa Baptist Church 31
From Callaway Gardens to Dacca to Serampore 39
From India to Callaway Gardens to Bangkok, Thailand ... 48
First Months Back in the States 57
New Orleans Baptist Seminary 66
First Baptist Church, Montezuma, Georgia 71
Back in the Kingdom of Thailand 79
Furloughing in the States 90
Stateside 102
First Baptist Church, ... 106
Bunkie, Louisiana 106
Montezuma Pastor Again 116
Beginning My Retirement Years 124
My Three Favorite Sermons 133

Introduction

I am writing this short story of myself for two reasons. The first, is that my children and grandchildren might know me better. They may see something of themselves in my story. They may learn from my successes and my failures. I write it for them because I love each one.

I am also writing this for me. I hope to see where I have come from and where I have gone. I hope to understand better who I am. But mostly I want to see where God has been at work in my life—whether I mention Him or not.

The title is very intentional. It is not simply "my story", but my story as I remember it. The two cannot be exactly the same. Our memories are faulty. They color events with shades that can confuse the details. I do have journals to fall back on beginning in 1977 when I was 29 years old. But those journals only record part of my story—the part, perhaps, I wanted to remember.

So, read this book with the understanding that it may not be all perfectly factual or true, but it is my story remembered.

1. Images from My Childhood

My earliest memories are from the only time my family lived in Huntsville, Alabama. I learned years later that my dad was receiving vocational training paid for by the government because of his service in the army during World War II. He studied dry cleaning which became his one and only profession for the rest of his life.

I can only guess that I was around 4 years old when we lived in a shot-gun style house with a long flight of concrete stairs leading up to the front door. My earliest memories are colored with fear. Two images appear.

The first is a big dark pantry off the kitchen. It made me nervous. I think we had mice! The second is when I was riding my tricycle on the sidewalk outside. Across the street was a three-legged Chihuahua. Like most Chihuahua dogs that I have ever encountered, this one had a nasty temper. It would bark at people walking along the sidewalk. I don't know that he ever bit anyone, but folks walked warily around it. Occasionally, the Chihuahua would notice me across the street innocently riding my tricycle. He barked at me. I don't remember him ever trying to cross the street, but the angry bark was enough. Inside the house I went.

Before I started school, we moved to 312 Albert Street, Albertville, Alabama. That was my home until I married at the age of 20. At the time, it had only two bedrooms and one bathroom. After my brother Tommy was born we eventually shared that second bedroom, except when I went off to college. I do remember as a teenager listening to my radio playing rock music softly under the covers. At night I could pick up WLS from Chicago. It was my favorite radio station. But I've gotten ahead of myself.

My earliest memory was my robbery—attempt. I had gotten two six-shooter toy guns for Christmas or my birthday. One afternoon, I hid behind the garbage cans. When a garbage truck pulled up, I jumped out and cried, "Stick 'em up!" They weren't impressed.

I remember playing with toy cars on our walk that led from the front porch to the road. I also enjoyed playing with little cowboys and Indians. And I had a friend, next door. His name was Kirby. He was a year younger than me. One day, when I was in the first grade, his mother, Mrs. Hearn, was a substitute teacher in my class. She brought Kirby with her. At some point we were not being quiet, and she paddled us both. It sort of set the pattern for my school life. I got at least one paddling from the first grade through at least the eighth grade. I was not a bad student. I just liked to talk!

One Christmas I got my first record player. It was, of course, only a small one that played the little 45s with one song on each side. I also, got a package of needles, because the needle on the record player had to be changed from time to time to keep it sharp. I recall that one of my first records was the song, "Duke of Earl" and another one was music by the Yardbirds. As mentioned earlier, at night, I could pick up WLS on my little radio, the rock station from Chicago. WVOK was the rock station in Birmingham.

My most memorable spanking took place in the eighth grade. It was an English class. We had a teacher new to the school. I assume she had transferred from another school. I do recall that on one occasion, we had to do a book report. I made up one. I made up the science fiction title, the characters, and the plot line. The main character was named Nomal Nworb—LaMon Brown backwards! Of course, I could have read a book. I loved reading and got books regularly from the town library. But I supposed this just seemed like fun. And I got away with it.

But that was not when I got that spanking. One day, a friend named Lawrence make a toy gun out of a piece of paper. I was sitting in the row next to him and behind him. He turned around and whispered my name. I looked up and he 'shot' me. I yelled and fell out of my seat. The teacher ran back to where I was and asked what happened. I raised my hand, pointed at Lawrence and said, "He shot me." Mrs. Garrison jerked me up, marched me to her desk, found her paddle, took me into the hall outside of our room and paddled me *until the bell rang*! Fortunately, this all occurred near the end of the period. Mrs. Garrison left our school after that one year and, honestly, I felt a little guilty. I hoped it wasn't because of me.

I am not sure when my interest in books started. I read some comic books as a child. Later, I discovered the old downtown Albertville Public Library. I remember walking there from my house and checking out books. Most of them were science fiction. (While my tastes in literature have expanded over the years, I usually still have a sci-fi book or two on my bookshelves waiting to be read.)

I'm also not sure when I began going to the movies. I recall one time, as a little boy, that Pop (mother's dad) and I walked to the movies together to see a Tarzan film. Later, I would work wrapping coat-hangers with paper at dad's dry-cleaning business to earn enough money to go to a Saturday movie and maybe buy a snack. The movie theater was downtown at that time just a block over from the dry-cleaning shop.

What about my family? I already mentioned my younger brother, Tom. We were separated by several years, so I don't remember a lot of interaction. Like me, he became a trumpet player in our high school band. He was a better musician than I. Later, he played bass guitar in a local rock band. After working at various jobs, he eventually became a youth and music director in several churches, eventually moving on to a long-time pastorate in a Baptist church in Gallant.

Bertha Idell Freeman Brown and Raymon Orsborne Brown were my parents. As I mentioned earlier, after World War II, my dad got some training to work in the dry-cleaning trade. This is what he did for the rest of his working life. Although he only had an 8th grade education, he was good at math, as I recall. My mom never worked full-time except as a homemaker, taking care of dad and her two sons. She worked part-time in some retail stores during the Christmas season and also worked in the school lunchroom for a short time. I was blessed with parents who loved me and cared for me.

My dad taught me about humility and faithfulness. My mom taught me about prayer and discipline. Pat has taught me about love and laughter.

9-3-14 I haven't gotten to Pat yet in my story, but the quote would have been incomplete without mention of some of what I learned from her.

Many years later, I read in a devotional book where the author prayed, "Thank you, Lord, for grandparents." I wrote, *of my dad's parents I only knew his mother, but she died when I was a teenager. She did not visit us often, but I do recall that she taught me how to eat milk-soaked crumbled up cornbread out of a glass. My mother's parents I knew much better since for many years they lived on the same street as us. I remember staying in their home as a boy when an ice-storm took out our electricity. They had a coal burning stove to heat the house. I also remember Pop putting wet snuff on a bumble bee sting I got on the bottom of my foot from jumping off of a sawhorse into a bed of clover. I don't remember any stories or words of wisdom from Pop and Freem, but I am thankful for them.* 9-13-15

The Beginnings of My Religious Life

The first church I remember is Mt. Calvary Baptist Church in Albertville, Alabama. My parents attended that church, and I was with them.

I remember the day my dad made a profession of faith or was converted. Actually, I remember what happened after we got home. He took the deck of 'poker' cards and tossed them in the heating stove that warmed our house. I don't think he ever gambled, but evidently he thought even having those cards was somehow wrong. It indicated to me the seriousness with which he took his new life in Christ. Some years later he came to understand that such cards could be used in acceptable ways.

Journal entry August 2006:

Yesterday in the Spirituality class we read a short section of Augustine's biography in which he spoke of his spiritual struggles and conversion. I asked them to write of their own conversion experience in their journals. I usually count mine from when I was around nine years old. I was in Vacation Bible School that summer. I don't recall any real crisis or sense of sin. This I remember. The pastor spoke on the final day during general assembly. He then invited us to the front and to accept Jesus. (I don't recall his actual words. I am guessing.) I do remember the boy sitting next to me asking me if we should walk to the front. I don't know if I said anything, but he went on to say that he was going—and he did. Then one of the teachers walked over to me and asked me if I didn't want to go to the front. I was always a fairly compliant boy, so I went with her. She probably asked me to pray, but at any rate we knelt together, and she prayed for my salvation. She asked me if I felt any different. (This may have been the second time after getting a negative response followed by more praying. I can't be sure.) Anyway, I said 'yes', but silently I thought, 'I guess'. The fact is that I did not have any great weight lifted or feel an overwhelming sense of joy. I really didn't feel all that different. I do recall telling my neighbor, Kirby, about being saved. And mom reminded me later that I had told another person. I suppose some folks might doubt the significance of that event as a moment of conversion. I know in later years I wondered about it as well. In many ways my accepting God's call to missions was a more emotional, volitional act following a period of struggle with the call. I have no doubts about being a child of God. I believe that event in VBS was part of my journey to Him. I don't know if that is when it began in terms of 'genuine' conversion or not. But I know where I am now. My sins are forgiven. Jesus is my Lord and Savior. The blessed Holy Spirit lives in me. By grace I am following God's will. I desire to love God and all that She has made. Thank You, loving Father. Thank You my Jesus. Thank You Spirit of God. Thank You. I praise Your Name. I worship You. I am no Augustine. But whatever I am, I belong to You. 9-16-06

Later, sometime in the 60s, E. J. Daniels brought his tent revival to Albertville. Most of the churches in town supported the revival effort. And I don't recall any blacks in the services. This was before integration. I was in my early teens.

For one night's invitation he encouraged those who doubted their salvation to come down. I did and with a number of other people were led into a side tent where we were met by counselors. Mine encouraged me to say the "sinner's prayer." I did, but again felt no different. Suddenly the girl being counseled near me had a highly emotional response and my counselor said, "Now, she's got it!" I've wondered later if he suspected that I did not.

It was during my college years, when I put to rest any doubts about my salvation. I finally realized that God's grace was far greater than my doubts. God had taken that little nine-year-old boy's heart and had begun to shape it into a heart that loved Jesus and all that he had come to teach and to do.

High School Years

Returning to my high school years, what was my life like after the 8th grade? Several things were important, or so it seems to my memory.

The first was my band life. I had begun to play in the bands of the Albertville school system when I was in the 5th grade. I began by playing trumpet. By the time I was in the 9th grade I was a member of the high school band.

I loved being in the band. I was not among the best of the trumpet players. Nor was I always on my best behavior at band practice. I recall one time when we were actually practicing on a baseball field. Mr. Nixon, our band director, was talking to one section of the band while we were standing in the formation we were to make as we would perform at half-time. I began, quietly, to pretend I was shooting birds as they flew over our heads. Suddenly, I heard Mr. Nixon yell at me, "LaMon, I see now why you're called monkey!!!" (Yes, that was my nickname—or one of them—as I was growing up.)

The second was girls, girls, girls! Actually, that could apply to most of my high school life. I was girl crazy. I recall two or three girls in the band whom I liked. When we would go on band trips, I would try to sit with them or close to them. However, nothing ever came from this attraction. I don't think I ever dated any of them.

During this time, I was working in the afternoon for my dad at his dry-cleaning plant. My main responsibility was picking up and delivering clothes. I only mention this because I often would drive a block or two out of my way to see if one or two of the girls might be outside the houses.

I also enjoyed concert season. After football season was over, we prepared for Christmas band programs, statewide band competitions, and a spring concert. During concert season three or four of us trumpeters played the French horn. I loved it. Even today, the sound of a French horn is beautiful to me.

Concerning academics, I was an above average student. I liked history best of all. Mr. Nixon, the band director, also taught some of the history classes. Of the 'math' classes, geometry was my favorite. I enjoyed debating in one of the English classes.

I don't have any vivid memories of classes, except for one. I took a physics class. I don't recall learning much physics, perhaps because in the Fall, the professor spent a good deal of each period talking about football—or so it seems to me now. I recall one day he was talking football (maybe about Joe Willie Namath—his favorite subject). Suddenly the principle appeared at the door and without skipping a beat, the professor pointed to something on the blackboard and began talking about physics.

My Story Remembered

Beginning My Life with Pat

Pat and I both grew up in Mt. Calvary Baptist Church of Albertville, Alabama. She is three years younger than me, so she noticed me before I noticed her. She tells the story that she knew at the age of 12 that I was the one she wanted to marry. It only took her five years to convince me!

We started 'going together' when I was a junior or senior in high school. We dated, went to the movies, sat together in church, went to youth events together, we held hands and kissed. We were normal teen-agers in love. Though truth be told, she was more in love with me than I was with her—at that time.

When I started college at Jacksonville State University, I broke it off with Pat. Guess I wanted to be free to meet college girls. Suffice it to say, it didn't work quite like that! So, eventually we got back together.

In the summer of 1968 on August 2, we were married. A high school friend of mine, Randy Smith, who had been licensed as a preacher performed our ceremony. Pat was 17 and I was 20. She was entering her Senior year at Albertville High and I was starting my Junior year at Samford University in Birmingham.

For our honeymoon, I had already taken my car to our motel to avoid getting it 'decorated' by friends. So, my dad drove us to Guntersville, ten miles away! We had a wonderful honeymoon, though much to my later embarrassment, I remember watching some football at one point. Pat loved me anyway—and for her love, I have ever more and more each year been thankful.

My Religious Life in High School and Early College

Repentance or rededication were still important parts of 'invitation' times in many churches in the 60s and 70s. I did my share. I don't remember ever confessing to a pastor about specific sins, but I do remember going to the front as the invitation hymn was being sung and either telling the pastor I wanted to rededicate my life to Christ or kneeling to pray at the front of our altarless church.

For what did I feel the need to repent? Shoplifting, drinking, and lust come to mind.

I remember stealing comic books from a store and a pack of playing cards from a different store. The last comic book theft was after I had just 'rededicated' my life the previous Sunday. I was almost immediately convicted and went back into the store and snuck the comic book back into the racks.

I grew up in a dry county, but there were bootleggers who brought alcohol from across the county line and sold them from their homes. I remember buying a bottle with a friend before going to a dance. I also remember driving across the county line into Madison County where it was legal to buy beer—though not by kids our age. Nevertheless, my friends knew a place that would sell to us. Because of the difficulty of buying booze, I rarely did it in high school, but did it enough to 'feel' guilty about it.

When I was attending Jacksonville, I would normally come home on the weekends. But one weekend I stayed at school to go to a weekend dance. Without going into details, I will simply say that my friends and I went to a pre-dance party where beer and wine and hard liquor was pretty prevalent. I never made it to the dance! I got wasted for the first time in my life. My friends drove me back to the dorm and deposited me on the top bunk. Sometime during the night, I rolled over and vomited all over the wall, then rolled back the other way and fell off the top bunk! That was my last drink for several years!

One final note, I do not believe that drinking in moderation is sinful. Getting drunk is, so that last time definitely was. And it was sinful for me to break the law and drink as an under-aged high schooler.

Then there is the sin of lust. If I have had a besetting sin this would be it. I mentioned earlier about being girl crazy. Eventually this turned to lustful thoughts. On several occasions I prayed to be released from this sin. And I repented of it as well. By God's grace and my commitment to Christ, I never committed fornication or adultery. Pat and I were virgins when we married. And I ever remain faithful to her.

Over the years I learned how to appreciate the beauty of females without having impure thoughts. God has blessed the creation of the human race with males and females. It is appropriate that we can be thankful for the human form without falling into sin.

During the winter break of that first year at Jacksonville, the youth group from Mt. Calvary attended an Alabama Baptist State Youth Convention. During that convention, a drawing to mission culminated

Some years earlier in high school, I was impressed in reading about Mahatmas Gandhi, the pacifist leader who secured India's independence from England. I learned about Gandhi while the war in Vietnam was raging in the 60s. I had already become convinced that pacifism was the clear teaching of Jesus in the Gospels—especially in Matthew 5. So, Gandhi became one of my early heroes.

One evening in a youth class at church, the material we were reading talked about different kinds of success. Gandhi was one of the illustrations. He was, the lesson said, a great success as a national leader, but not a success spiritually because he never became a baptized Christian. My response was anger. I got MAD that someone was denigrating my hero. This anger seethed for days. Eventually, the anger was transformed into a concern for the millions in India who had never heard the story of Jesus Christ.

During an extended invitation time at that State Youth Convention, I went forward accepting God's call to be a missionary to India. Shortly after that I made the same public affirmation at our home church.

Two side notes:

First, Pat, unbeknownst to me, had made a similar commitment to missions at an earlier church service at Mt. Calvary. I suppose I was absent from that service. Her commitment was not as specific as mine, but it was a commitment to be a missionary. So, even before we were married, we felt God leading us to overseas mission.

Second, I still think the author of that lesson was wrong. I fully expect to meet Gandhi in glory. One of my favorite hymns is *There's a Wideness in God's Mercy* by Frederick Faber:

There's a wideness in God's mercy, like the wideness of the sea;
There's a kindness in His justice, which is more than liberty.
There is welcome for the sinner, and more graces for the good;
There is mercy with the Savior; there is healing in His blood.
But we make His love too narrow by false limits of our own;
And we magnify His strictness with a zeal He will not own.
For the love of God is broader than the measure of one's mind;
And the heart of the Eternal is most wonderfully kind.

If our love were but more simple, we could take Him at His word; And our lives would be more loving in the likeness of our Lord.

College Years and Early Married Life

Since I had accepted a call to missions, I transferred to Samford University in Birmingham. As student preparing for ministry, I received a good break on the tuition. I lived in Crawford Johnson Hall—a male dormitory. The first semester I had a roommate, but he was rarely there. The second semester I had the room to myself.

Now for a few memories, with the caveat that I can't be sure all of these occurred in my sophomore year. Some may have been later.

Although I transferred from Jacksonville, I maintained history as my major with a double minor in religion and English. My favorite teacher was Dr. Wayne Flynt. I remember visiting in his office a time or two when I had some questions. He was always warm and welcoming. It was to no one's surprise that he won an award one year as the favorite teacher of the year—as voted by the students.

One story: I took a class with him entitled Intellectual History in America. We had a textbook to read and his lectures to listen to. He told us that the final exam, which counted for 50% of our grade, would be on one chapter in the book and on our notes from his lectures. A friend and I decided we would each read half the book—one of us the odd chapters and one the even chapters. Then we would get together and help each other study. There was an uneven number of chapters, so we decided simply to omit reading the chapter on architecture—makes sense, right? I mean who would ask the one question from that chapter? Of course, that was the chapter. When the exams were passed out, I actually laughed out loud. Well, I failed that exam and got my only D in college. But still, I loved Dr. Flynt.

He was a scholar, a wonderful teacher, and a fine Christian man.

Pranks at Crawford Johnson were an ongoing activity. For my birthday, some of the guys kidnapped me. I was only wearing undershorts. The put me in the trunk of a car, drove me up the hill to the girl's dormitories, and let me out to walk back to our dorm. I could hear the squeals of delight from the girls. Fortunately, they kidnapped me without my glasses, so I couldn't see anyone clearly. I simply sauntered back to our dorm and went to bed.

The War in Vietnam was raging while I was in college. Being a pacifist, I was opposed to the war. So, you can imagine my consternation when the government instituted a draft that would use a lottery system based on our birthdates to decide who would be first to be drafted. I am forever thankful that my number came out very high, so I escaped the horrors of that senseless war.

One time we had either a military man or a government politician to come and speak at a general assembly. The school administration warned the students that any protest or walkouts would be subject to immediate expulsion. However, the administration also did a clever thing. They had the much-admired Dr. Flynt to introduce the speaker. He encouraged us to listen respectfully as we would want others to listen to us. It worked, there were no demonstrations or walkouts.

We did have one hippy at Samford. I remember he would go to rooms and write "Give Peace a Chance" on the blackboards. I never knew who he was, but I admired him.

I loved college, as I would love seminary. I could have been a career student! I loved research and writing papers. So, my memories of college and seminary are mostly colored with happy hues.

As I mentioned earlier, Pat and I were married on August 2, 1968. I was 20; she had just turned 17. She completed her senior year as a married woman. She was not the only married person in her class. There were at least three others.

Our first place together was half a house. It had been divided for two families. There were no connecting doors between the two parts. Ours was kind of shotgun: living room, bedroom, kitchen—yes, you had to walk through our bedroom to get to the kitchen! Our rent was $25 a month.

The first year of our marriage was a hectic one. Pat went to high school and did some chores around the house, including cooking. I worked 4 days a week for my dad at the dry cleaners. I preached on Sundays at a mission sponsored by Mt. Calvary Baptist Church. I took a full load at Samford University—two days a week, 8 am to 8 pm.

To make my 8 am class, I had to leave the house by 6 or a little after. Pat would get up and fix me a wonderful breakfast—eggs, bacon, and biscuits. She did this until I confessed that that early in the morning, I really wasn't very hungry. What was I thinking!!???

After Pat graduated we moved to the married student apartments at Samford for my senior year. During that year I think I had four different part-time jobs. Two were at dry cleaners. One was a night job at a bank where Pat also worked. The other was a youth director's position at a church in south Alabama.

I was youth director for about one month—maybe two. The pastor wanted me to teach the youth on Wednesday nights. I gave them some options about what they might want to discuss from a biblical perspective. They chose race-relations. This was in 1969 or 70. We had made some strides in better relations, but much still needed to be done. I was excited for the opportunity to teach the youth on this vital topic. The chairman of the deacons and the pastor were not so enthralled. I was let go; guess you could say I was fired.

I had planned to go to seminary after graduation. I had already been accepted at Southeastern Baptist Seminary. But one day, we got a brochure in the mail from Golden Gate Baptist Seminary. I asked Pat what she thought about us going to Golden Gate. She thought it was a great idea, so that is what we did. What an adventure!

To Golden Gate and Back Again

We drove west in our 1960s Volkswagen Beetle. We did ship some stuff by train, but still our little Bug was loaded. The trip was planned for four nights and five days. The plan worked! We stayed at three motels and one night with some relatives of Pat's family.

What do I remember about the trip?

1) It was exciting. We were two young people traveling on an adventure.

2) The little Volkswagen had no air-conditioning. We could open the little corner front windows to have the wind blow on us. Unfortunately, in the southwest, the wind was all hot!

3) We did have some car trouble. Eventually, a mechanic showed me how to reattach a switch under the hood that would come loose. When that happened and we stopped, the car would go dead. That made traveling up the hills of San Francisco a scary challenge. But we made it with no problems.

4) I recall trying to pass big rigs on four lane highways. As I would get near the front of the truck, the wind whipping around the truck would halt the little Bug and we would have to get back behind it. However, I did learn how to draft behind them.

5) Although I kept the accelerator on the floor (going about 60 as I recall), it was not unusual for big, powerful cars to pass us. However, we had the last laugh as we went up the Eastern side of the Rockies. We passed several of those cars who had pulled over to get water for their over-heated engines. Our little air-cooled VW engine just puttered along.

6) When we drove into San Diego, I smelled the salt water of the Pacific Ocean for the first time. It was a wonderful experience.

7) We got near the campus of Golden Gate on Sunday evening, so we found a motel and stayed there. We called home to tell our parents of our safe arrival. We were wearing shorts, as we had the whole trip. We called from a phone booth that was open around the bottom. Friends, it is not warm in San Francisco in the early Summer! The cold wind was blowing into that phone booth and we could hear our teeth chattering.

We loved our 13 months in California. It was one of the most formative times of our lives. We were removed from family and old friends. We had only ourselves. I suspect that it made us closer than having stayed in the South would have. We had to depend on one another.

In addition to going to school, I had three different jobs at three different times. First, I worked on the grounds crew of the seminary. Shortly after getting to the seminary, I took an IQ test. My score was the highest of any of the entering students. How smart was I? Well one day, I managed to get a finger clipped by a lawn mower blade as I 'carefully' tried to remove some wet grass stuck in the exit part of the mower—without turning the mower off!! Fortunately, the injury was very minor.

The second job I had was working for another student who had started a cleaning company. The company was composed of us two guys. He had contracts to clean a restaurant and bar at night and to clean at an apartment building. Along the way we also did some inside house painting.

The third job was music and youth director of El Sobrante Baptist Church in El Sobrante, California. I don't know how good I was at either part of that job title. I do remember one time singing a rare solo as the special music. Afterwards one of the members told me how much courage it must have taken—hmmmm!??!

I enjoyed being music director, but probably enjoyed being the youth director even more. We had Bible study and fellowship times in homes after church. We also went on 'mission' trips. Once or twice, we drove over to Sausalito for the day. In the mid to late 60s, Sausalito was not yet primarily a tourist spot. It was still full of hippies. We would go there, sing some songs in a park and then split up to hand out tracts or just to talk with folks. It was a fun time and hopeful a good experience for the youth and for those who heard us sing.

In becoming a staff member at El Sobrante, we felt the need to move from the seminary to be closer to the church and the youth. We rented an apartment. This meant I had to drive across a bridge north of Tiburon to get to the seminary. On really windy days, the old Volkswagen would tremble crossing the water.

The other means of support that we had was occasionally house sitting mostly while we were living at the seminary. Often when people wanted to go on vacation they would hire a student to stay at their house until they returned. Sometimes, it also involved taking care of their children as well. Perhaps our favorite house was one in Tiburon that looked out over the water. We could sit in front of a big picture window and watch the fog come in over the waters. It was awesome.

The most significant event of our time in California was on June 27, 1971. On that day, we were blessed (as I had predicted!) with a little red-headed baby girl. Karina Renee Brown was born in a hospital in San Rafael. The name Karina comes from the Greek word *karis* which means "grace". I had wanted to name her Hesedh, which is the Hebrew word for "loving kindness". Knowing that our daughter would forever be called "Hessy", my sweet wife put her foot down—so Kari it was. I think she is grateful!

At some point in 1971, we realized that we needed to return to Alabama. We were still planning on being missionaries and as my wife, Pat would need at least two years of college to be appointed as a career missionary. Returning to Alabama and going to a junior college promised to be much less expensive in the long run. Additionally, Pat shared with me that God had spoken to her about going home. So, with God's directions and practical concerns related to our missionary calling, we moved back to Albertville.

How smart was I? Well, I convinced a mechanic to hook up a small trailer to the back of our little Volkswagen. It was filled with our worldly goods, including boxes of books. We were spending the last night with one of our church families—the Sealys. Fortunately, as we drove to their house, Mr. Sealy noticed how heavy the trailer was and said that we could not attempt the trip that way. So, we unloaded all the books and some other items. The Sealys promised to ship them to us—which they did, free of charge. All I can say is "thank God" for his wisdom and kindness. Even with a much lighter load, climbing the Rocky Mountains on the way out of California, I still had to drive a lot of the way in first and second gear! We would never have gotten over those mountains with the original load.

Needless to say, when we arrived back in Albertville, our parents were thrilled. I suspect they were most thrilled about that beautiful grandbaby, but that was okay too.

Beulah Baptist Church, Albertville, and the Charismatic Movement

Returning to Albertville, I had to get a job. I went to work at Bryant's Furniture Manufacturing Company. I was one of two cushion stuffers. The work was exactly as it sounds. Cushions that had been sewn in one part of the plant came to us and we had to stuff kapok into each cushion—making sure all the corners were full. I lost the hair on my right arm, but I have to say that I enjoyed the work. My co-worker was a funny guy.

Pretty soon, I was hired as the youth director at Beulah Baptist Church. (I had preached at a youth revival there sometime earlier.) Beulah is a country church. Some youth attended Albertville schools, while others were in Boaz. Pat and I had a great time with them. We had Bible studies and fellowships in our home. One of the youth (Joanie Miller) became a pastor's wife and has a ministry of her own. Another one (Mike Johnson) became a church planter and pastor. Others, as they grew up, also became active in churches. Others sadly did not. Such is the reality of youth ministry.

With several of the youth I started a singing group. We called ourselves Nephesh Hayah which is Hebrew for "living souls". We sang at Beulah and at other events. It was quite fun. I pretended to play a harmonica!

It was during this time that our baby boy was born. Jason LaMon came into the world on February 8, 1973. Whereas Kari was an easy baby, Jason made up for it! However, it wasn't all his fault. He apparently came home from the hospital with thrush in his mouth—a kind of fungus. It made it painful for him to eat. The doctor prescribed some medicine, but days went by and he still suffered from it.

There were certain individuals who were said to be able to heal thrush. I forget what they were called. Anyway, after one visit to the doctor, he said, *perhaps* kidding that maybe we should find one of these persons. Pat's mom, Mildred, knew of one. They took the little baby to this person, who then took Jason into a room alone. Shortly, he returned with Jason. They brought him home and his thrush quickly cleared up. Years later I talked with a nurse friend and she suggested that the person had probably put saliva into the mouth of Jason, because for certain cases, saliva has some healing properties. Whatever the case, we were thankful.

The charismatic movement was going strong during this time. This Christian movement emphasized being baptized with the Holy Spirit (a second experience after conversion) and speaking in tongues. They were not connected with the older Pentecostal movement. They tended to be less restrictive concerning how their members could participate in modern culture.

A charismatic church began in a storefront on Main Street in Albertville. The promises of the movement intrigued me. I had long been interested in stories of spiritual experiences like those recorded in the Bible and found in other religions. Pat's sister, Jonnie, was the first in our extended family to speak in tongues. She became, for a while, active in the movement. At some point, through Jonnie's encouragement, Pat also spoke in tongues. Perhaps because I was not against the movement and had a non-judgmental attitude in general, Jonnie told me she thought I had already received the baptism in the Holy Spirit but had just not yet spoken in tongues.

One day, I went to the house of one of the leaders of this new church. There he led me to speak in tongues. He laid hands on me and asked me to start making sounds with my mouth. I did.

Suddenly, I was no longer in control. I was "speaking in tongues". This experience is called ecstatic which basically means out of body. I recall being able to see myself speaking in tongues as though I were above my body.

The result of this experience was two-fold. I had a great sense of peace. And I lost my ministry at Beulah. Most of the churches in our area were fearful of the charismatic movement. They feared losing members and they feared churches being split over the issue. Beulah was no different. I had begun to teach the youth on the Holy Spirit in the New Testament, though I was not interested in leading anyone to speak in tongues. When the parents and pastor found out about my experience and what I was teaching, my welcome there began to change.

The chair of the deacons and father of three of the youth came to my house and talked with me. The pastor also came and talked. Neither were ugly or mean-spirited, but the writing was on the wall. I would also mention that my parents were upset as well. They asked one or two people they knew to visit me—which they did.

It was at this point that Pat and I decided it was time to return to my seminary education. I don't know how impactful my charismatic experience and subsequent negativity from the church contributed to that decision, but I am certain it mattered. Without that experience and subsequent events, I don't know when or if we would have moved back to a seminary. I assume we would, but don't know when it might have been. It is interesting how events contribute to the decisions we make.

I will revisit the charismatic movement later in this rambling book of remembrances, but I will say that 1) I have never believed that the baptism of the Holy Spirit is a one-time second experience after conversion, 2) speaking in tongues is not mandated for all Christians, 3) speaking in tongues is found in non-Christian settings, so there may be, at least partially, a psychological reason for its appearance, 4) speaking in tongues is only an experience given by God if it increases one's capacity to love.

Over the years I have wondered if my experience was of divine origin or psychologically produced. I have gone back and forth on answering that question. Suffice it to say, I don't know! But that is okay. 'Spiritual' experiences are by their very nature not easily susceptible to rational explanations. I have never regretted speaking in tongues that one time, but I have never encouraged others to seek that experience. I don't think the experience made me either a better or a worse Christian.

My Story Remembered

New Orleans and Tangipahoa Baptist Church

While I had hoped to return to Golden Gate someday, moving to California with two additional family members made it much more daunting. So, we decided to go to another multicultural city for seminary training. We were still aiming toward missions overseas.

In the summer of 1973, we moved into an upstairs apartment on the campus of New Orleans Baptist Theological Seminary. We had been married for 5 years, but we had never owned an air-conditioner. I think we lasted maybe two days in that steamy apartment before buying one!

I will mention that at some point in our first year or two there, Jason managed to get out of our front door and tumble down the stairs falling to the landing between floors. He was not really injured at all, but it began a pattern that will appear over and over again in the next 10 or 15 years. Every time we moved, he managed to get into an accident and hurt himself. He was a rambunctious handful! Might as well get them all out of the way: Tangipahoa, fell onto edge of concrete walkway stepping across a corner from church to education hall—stitches; Bangladesh, fell up the stairs at school—stitches; Serampore, playing a running game at night and ran into a clothesline—stitches; Bangalore, running with some other mks and crashed into a wall; Bangkok, ran through a plate class window—emergency room visit where most of the glass fragments were removed! There may have been others, but this is the best my memory has. (Sorry I don't have more Kari stories, but she was less adventurous.)

I loved our time in New Orleans and at the seminary. The seminary provided daycare for student children to allow spouses to work and students to study. Pat and I both got jobs at a place called Surgico. It was a surgical supply company. Pat became the assistant secretary, and I became the delivery person. I delivered surgical supplies to hospitals all over the New Orleans area. It was a great way to get to know that wonderful city.

Pat and I had some great experiences in New Orleans. We would occasionally go to a big mall that had a Cineplex. We would see two movies and have a meal—really make a day of it. We also had a chance to go to a couple of concerts. One was by Kris Kristofferson. But my all-time favorite was the concert with Linda Ronstadt—the heart throb of many a young man during those days. She was the second act. The final act was a singer I had not yet learned to appreciate—Willie Nelson. I was hooked!

At Golden Gate I had not been a great student. I played way too much ping pong, but I did get the Asian ping pong paddle grip down pat! However, perhaps because I was a bit more mature, I took my studies more seriously at NOBTS. At Golden Gate, I had loved Hebrew studies and was fascinated by the spiritual experiences of the Old Testament saints. So, I had thought I might major in Old Testament and Hebrew. However, by the time we moved to New Orleans, I had been out of school for two years and had not kept up my Hebrew studies. So, I feared I would be too far behind. I chose instead to turn to Systematic Theology and have never regretted the decision.

My first theology course was taught by Dr. Fisher Humphreys. He quickly became my favorite of all the teachers at New Orleans. I had him for several classes both in the M.Div. program and in the doctoral program. I eventually became his grader or 'fellow'. I even got to teach a class or two for him when he was out of town. His influence on me cannot be overestimated. That does not mean we always agreed or agree on everything, but I learned much from him both in terms of theological content and how to do and teach theology. He became a fast friend whom I have enjoyed staying in close contact with over these many years.

My other favorite professor was Dr. James Mosteller. He was one of two church history professors at that time. Dr. Mosteller had a broader denominational background than many of the professors there. He had taught in an American Baptist institution in Chicago. It was through him and particular his course entitled Devotional Classics that the direction of my studies was determined. While I had heard of Christian mystics in an introductory church history class at Golden Gate, it was Dr. Mosteller's influence that enabled me to get a foothold in that wonderful area of spirituality. Unfortunately, he died suddenly when I was in the doctoral program.

In 1975, I was called to pastor my first church. It was Tangipahoa Baptist Church in Tangipahoa, Louisiana. The church had a history of hiring professors or doctoral students as their pastor. We moved into the parsonage and stayed for about three and a half years.

Remember El Sobrante? That was where I served as youth and music director. It is a Spanish phrase meaning "the left-overs". Tangipahoa was from an Indian word that mean "cob of corn". For years I noted that I had gone from the leftovers to the corncobs and wasn't sure if that was moving up or down!

But like El Sobrante, Tangipahoa was a laboratory for learning. It was there where I had my first funerals and my first weddings. It was there where I had the thrill of my first baptisms and the confusion of losing some church members. It was there that I learned the discipline I would need in the years ahead. I preached twice on Sundays and had a Bible study on Wednesday nights. I also prepared the Sunday bulletins, including running them off on an old-fashioned mimeograph machine. All the while I was involved in doctoral studies at New Orleans. I also coached the women's softball team. (Pat played first base!) And I played right field for our men's softball team.

We had one crisis during our time in Tangipahoa. Jason became seriously ill with some strange lung infection. It happened several times. He would get sick, go to the hospital, come home, and get sick again. Allergies were probably one of the issues. So, we removed stuffed animals from his room and went from feather pillows to foam-filled ones. In spite of that, he was back in the hospital where he stayed for weeks—even celebrating his 3rd birthday there. His condition was not getting better. The doctors eventually had him on the strongest antibiotic that they could use. After that terrible scare, he recovered and came home. The doctors thought at one time that perhaps he had Legionnaires Disease. But later it was suggested that he had an immature or slowly developing immune system. I thought this might explain the trouble with thrush as a baby. Anyway, he eventually outgrew whatever the problems were and became a healthy vibrant boy.

In December of 1977 I began one of the more important practices of my whole life. I began to keep a journal. Nothing has helped me more to pay attention to my reading in the Bible and other books. Nothing has helped me more to pay attention to what was going on in the days of my life. These gains were not immediately apparent in those early years of journaling, but eventually I found my bearings and became better at it.

One of my first entries from December 23, 1977, *Jason is coming down with the chicken pox. . .. But he is doing fine so far. Pat and I fussed today over X-mas spending. I was tired and she probably was too, but still no excuses. Must pray more tomorrow. Help me Lord.* Yearly Christmas spending continued to be a source of conflict over the years. My sweetheart was always the more generous one!

Four items from this time.

First, Pat and I had made friends with Chip and Martha Sloan who lived near us in New Orleans. Chip and I were in the M.Div. program together. We also were members of the same church in New Orleans.

After I went to Tangipahoa, I helped Chip to find a pastorate in a neighboring town. For better or for worse, Chip gets credit for introducing me to golf! He was an excellent player. There was a course in a nearby town where pastors could play at a discount. So, that is what we did. I loved playing there with him and with other friends.

I remember one 'funny' story. Three of us were playing one day when storm clouds began to appear. I kept saying, "Don't worry. It will go around us." It didn't. We huddled up in an open-air shelter—mostly posts and a ceiling. We were keeping dry, but a lightning strike hit a tree next to the building. Chip, who was wearing metal cleats, felt the electricity run through his shoes. He was not hurt, but we could see the scar on the tree where the lightning had run down it into the ground.

Second, was another friendship that was formed when I was in the doctoral program. Gerald Wright was pastoring a church in a neighboring association. Since we were both studying for degrees in Systematic Theology, we were able to begin riding together regularly to seminars on campus. So, Gerald and Kathy Wright became life-long friends. Eventually the four of us became missionaries with the Foreign Mission Board of the SBC.

Whereas, Chip and I were often on different sides of theological discussions, Gerald and I were like two peas in a pod. We shared many of the same viewpoints and eventually both became interested in spirituality and the classic Christian mystics.

And that brings me to my third point—my doctoral studies and dissertation. I mentioned earlier my broad introduction to

Christian mysticism in Dr. Mosteller's class. Later when I began my doctoral studies I had an advantage over many other doctoral students. I already knew the focus of my dissertation—Christian mysticism. In every seminar I took, I managed to write papers on specific mystics or some topic that could be related to mysticism. So, by the time I finished those seminars I had built up an impressive bibliography and notes that would help me in writing my dissertation.

I must be careful not to neglect [our] kids during this time. They need my attention. Of course, I must have time for Pat and me too! Things are rather hectic and probably will be for another three or four weeks. August 1978

The title I chose for my doctoral dissertation in Systematic Theology was *The Doctrine of God in Nineteenth and Twentieth Century English Mysticism as Found in Baron Friedrich von Hugel, Evelyn Underhill, and William Inge.* The problem I set out to prove was that specific Christian mystics had orthodox understandings of God. (This had been debated, especially by those who were suspicious of the mystics.) I must say that I loved researching for and writing this dissertation. The truth is that in seminary I always enjoyed doing research papers, so this dissertation, while far from being an easy project, was one of the more enjoyable activities of my academic life. I graduated in December of 1978 with a doctorate in Systematic Theology. (Pat graduated with her bachelor's degree from Southeast Louisiana University in the same month. She got a degree in Education with a focus on Special Education—a degree that would be very helpful in years to come.)

Our pet poodle was killed by a car this afternoon. Very tearful for Pat and the kids. I feel sad too. He was a really good puppy. Two things about pets: 1) Our attachment for pets should be but a shadow of our concern and compassion for human beings. But it often isn't. 2) The joy and even communion that we have because of and with the higher pets encourage me in thinking that our perfected joy and sharing of life in glory will include at least some of the animal kingdom. Feb. 1978

The fourth item was getting ready to move on to the next stage of our journey.

As I neared graduation (and Pat too), moving on seemed to be the next step. I had three or four pastor search committees visit but was not called by any of them.

At one point I noted that I was attracted to working in the northwest, but actually I met with a representative from the northeast about pastoring there. In addition, Fisher suggested I might check out teaching possibilities, specifically at the Baptist seminary in Mexico. I did talk to a person about that. Additionally, I had sent my resume to a large number of Baptist colleges and seminaries hoping to get a teaching position. (Only two bothered to respond and neither had openings.)

In early 1979, I read of openings for missionaries with the Foreign Mission Board of the SBC.

Received forms from Foreign Mission Board. Among them was a job description for a teaching position at Serampore College in India! It is almost like a dream come true, because my first interest was in India many years ago [when I felt called to missions]. Of course, the future is still cloudy and hidden from view, so I do not know what the outcome of all of this may be. Jan. 1979

Pat is eating at the flower club tonight. She continues to grow more attractive and confident almost daily. I am so fortunate. Jan. 1979

Nothing out of the ordinary has happened since Wednesday. Jason was six on Thursday. I guess that was 'out of the ordinary'. He had not been six before! Feb. 1979

We had been in touch with a church in Massachusetts. At the same time, we were dealing with the Foreign Mission Board about India. Days after we were appointed by the Board as missionaries, the church extended a call to us. We turned it down, since we had already made a commitment to the work in India. How different would our life been had the church called us first. (We were appointed to India on July 10, 1979.)

Today is Pat's birthday. She burned her finger cooking breakfast—hopefully not too bad. I bought her some candy. Aug. 1979

Journal entry about our last Sunday in Tangipahoa:

Sunday was a good day. Morning sermon on Christian Letters was good. . .. Baptized four. Had fellowship dinner. Observed the Lord's Supper at night. Finished the study in Philippians with adults in Church Training. It was very appropriate as Paul was telling the church at Philippi that they, because of their gifts to him, were receiving credit in the victories of his ministry. Tangipahoa will receive such credit in any good work I perform on the mission field."

From Callaway Gardens to Dacca to Serampore

I have to mention how much we loved our time at missionary orientation in Callaway Gardens. It was wonderful. We were there for three months. We learned a lot about what being a missionary entailed. We made many friends. Jason learned to ride a bike. I played a lot of golf. Pat was hit with our colleagues—especially those who drove the bus for our kids to go to school. She gave them freshly baked buttermilk biscuits! Both Kari and Jason made some good friends.

Several side notes:

1. Pat and I visited the Episcopal Church where Ben and Lynn Alford attended in Columbus. (Ben was a childhood friend of mine from Albertville.) That was my first experience of Episcopal worship, liturgy, and Holy Communion. It was the beginning of a lifelong appreciation of Anglicanism. While two of my dissertation persons had been Anglican, this was my first time to worship in that tradition.

2. In addition, to attending classes at MOC (Missionary Orientation Center), I had other responsibilities including writing a paper and a book review for the Theological Educator (of New Orleans Baptist Seminary), preparing a lecture on the charismatic movement in the Catholic Church which I was to share with our colleagues, and preparing sermons to preach in Selma, Alabama (where friends Philip and Cynthia Wise were) and in Albertville at our home church.

3. We got word from the Board that we could go to Dacca, Bangladesh for three months on a tourist visa. This was necessitated by the need of Serampore College to get our housing in order.

I do not know when I have been so moved to tears. Leaving so many great friends (maybe for this life) was (and is) sad beyond words. If I were really a poet, I would write a poem to the tears of parting. 12-12-79

After a nice day or two stay in Hawaii, we arrived in Dacca, Bangladesh on January 15, 1980.

Being a new missionary on the field is always a time for unexpected discoveries. One of my first was an attempt to write one of our new missionary friends from Orientation. When I went to mail a letter to them, I was told that letters to Israel could not be sent from Bangladesh.

A few days after being in Dacca, we got up one morning, blew our noses and our handkerchiefs were filled with black discharge. It scared us until we realized it was due to the air quality in the city. Maybe we should still have been frightened!

We began to study Bengali which is the language of Bangladesh and in our ultimate destination—Calcutta and West Bengal. (The modern name is Kolkata, but I will use the name in vogue at the time we were there.) I enjoyed the language study, but neither Pat nor I became very proficient in Bengali—in large part because my teaching at Serampore was in English. One of the few lines I still remember went something like "amar stri dek ben na." It means, "don't look at my wife." I don't think I ever used it, but I wanted too from time to time. Among the Bengalis it was assumed that all western women were morally loose, so looks, touches and pinches could be fairly common. I don't remember Pat getting either of the last two—which was fortunate for them in light of my sweetheart's Irish heritage.

We met some Norwegian missionaries studying language with us. They were very friendly and kind. This was true of most if not all the Scandinavians we met over the years.

There is a very pretty Bengali girl (maybe in her teens) who sells flowers outside the gate of the American Club. I buy from her, but I am afraid to talk with her because of Muslim restrictions. Pat wants to as well and may the next time we see her. 3-12-80 (Visions of her haunted me long after we left Dacca. I have no idea if she ever heard the Gospel or not. I pray God's mercy for her.)

Four notes:

1. I was reminded of the importance of prayer in Bangladesh. It was about the only form of ministry I could do. So, I attempted to be diligent.

2. We discovered that Jason was standing next to the compound wall and exchanging money with Bengalis who passed by—his American money for their Bangladeshi money. We had to put a stop to that!

3. I played golf once in Dacca. We each had to use two caddies—one to carry our clubs and one known as the fore-caddy. He would go down the fairway and wait for us to hit the ball. The he would go to it, so we would know where it was. They were bare-footed and very good at picking up the balls with their toes and moving them further down the fairway. Their reasoning: golfers with good scores would tip better!

4. On the roof of the guest house crows gathered. They were the biggest I had ever seen! They were not particularly afraid of people. They would sit there and stare at us. A bit unnerving!

Our Bangladeshi visa expired before our Indian visa was given. So, we went to Thailand for a wonderful month. We arrived in Bangkok on the 15th. We certainly appreciated the air-conditioning, the department stores, and the friendliness of the Thais.

A couple of weeks afterwards, we went to a wonderful missionary resort called The Juniper Tree. I played golf with clubs borrowed from new friend, Jack Kinnison who we had met with his wife Lynn in Bangkok at the guesthouse.

Our time there was mostly idyllic: swimming, shell-hunting, eating, and playing table games with other missionary families who were staying there.

Jason managed to get stung by a small jelly fish, but quickly recovered his composure and fearlessness.

Kari leaned on a sink and it broke from the wall! She was embarrassed. The lady manager was upset but wasn't ugly about it.

Our Indian visas came through and we arrived in Calcutta on April 16, 1980. We took two taxis with kids and luggage to Serampore.

Sitting out on the patio of our upstairs apartment, I enjoyed looking at the Hoogley River, the foliage, and the birds. We also had one semi-tamed monkey named Sittaram who would enter the house if we left doors or windows open. One time we heard Jason screaming in his bed. Sitaram had come for a visit!

Within a couple of weeks of our arrival in Serampore, we made a trip to Bangalore in southern India to meet the rest of our missionary colleagues. We met Gail Hill among them who became a life-long friend. We saw our first movie in Bangalore during that visit. It was Star Wars!

Our trip to Calcutta was expensive. We bought too much, soccer ball, milk boiler, tea service, food, magazines, birds & chipmunks & accessories & a puppy. Only one chipmunk survived a full week with us! All the rest died, except the parrot who escaped. 6-18-80

Life was simple in those days. We had an Indian cook and a cleaning lady who sort of went with the apartment. I enjoyed listening to Armed Forces Radio on our shortwave radio. I heard the Indigo Girls for the first time. And baseball games were fun to listen to. UNO and Parcheesie were games of choice among our family. We played almost every day. I did some latch-hook designs on cloth. I'm sure Pat's were better!

I am up earlier that the rest this morning and am enjoying the soft rain and birds as I sit on the veranda. I guess even hemorrhoids have their good side! HA! 6-26-80

One of our missionary colleagues teaching at the college was a former medical doctor from Scotland. He helped me understand how to treat those hemorrhoids, which, as far as I can remember, was the first time I had had problems with them.

For the last few days, I have not felt just right but yesterday [with our cook being gone for a day], Pat fixed some iced tea and it felt so good. Then we had beef stew for lunch and pineapple sandwiches for supper. It was really great. Perhaps the coldness and the unspiced nature of the meals was helpful. I have enjoyed Indian food, but maybe the heat and it together was not agreeing with me. 7-14-80

Very early on, I began to have problems with itching. It was worse whenever it rained. Before going to bed, I would shower and would have difficulty getting to sleep. I itched like crazy! I could only guess that I was having a reaction to the nearby jute factory whose smoke poured over the campus.

Pat's main responsibility was to teach our kids. However, eventually Kari began to have some problems—not with school, but with life around her. She looked mature for her age and could not escape the unwelcomed attention of Bengali males. She became more withdrawn. This led to the hard decision for her to stay with the Van and Sarah Williams in Bangalore and go to the English language school there.

I enjoyed my teaching at Serampore. It was one of the only places where I actually taught Systematic Theology which was my major in seminary. I did discover that the American approach to theology was not as helpful in the Indian setting. Theology was learned better with stories and images than with rational explanations. I tried to teach in the following years (wherever we were) in a more contextualized way.

Pat and I had concerns about remaining in Serampore. We hated being away from Kari. The lack of a church setting for spiritual growth—especially for Jason—concerned us. There was also the issue of where I could have the best use of my abilities in a mission setting.

In addition to teaching, we did other things that showed the love of Christ. We used part of our tithe to have the windows and verandas of the married student apartments screened, especially for the safety of the babies.

Pat and Jason distributed Christmas presents for some babies, children, and our servants yesterday. 11-26-80

Pat and Jason left for Bangalore a few days before me, as I stayed in Serampore to finish the term.

Today's the day [I go to Bangalore]. I have really missed my family, especially Pat. . . . I have felt a deep vacancy in my life which is the place Pat fills. There is nothing sacrilegious in saying that it is a vacancy only Pat can fill. God has made us for himself, but he has also made me for Pat and Pat for me—and my heart is restless without her presence. 12-9-80

We eventually finished our ministry in Serampore and moved to South India where I would begin teaching at South India Biblical Seminary in the little town of Bangarapet. With students from all over India attending there, my teaching continued to be in English. We arrived in Bangarapet on April 5, 1981.

On the 12th we went to the constitution of a new Telugu language church in Bangarapet. The service was inspiring, but over two hours long. We enjoyed holding some of the babies. Since diapers were not in use, one of us came home with pee stains!

South India Biblical Seminary was definitely different from Serampore. It was more evangelical and conservative. I liked to tell people I went from being the most conservative member of the faculty to the most liberal one—without changing any of my beliefs. Such was the difference between Serampore and SIBS.

SIBS was a Weslyan Methodist school in the Arminian camp. They rejected the idea of predestination taught by Calvin and his followers. They also believed in a second experience of grace that had been taught by John Wesley—an experience that enabled believers to live a life devoid of *intentionally* disobeying God. However, they rejected the Pentecostal idea of speaking in tongues. I fit in well since even in college I had done a paper on Wesley's perfectionism and Matthew 5:48, in general agreeing with his understanding. And I was convinced an Arminian—believing in free-will and that God does not force anyone to be saved.

Pat, with a little help from me, finished the kid's tree houses yesterday. 5-21-81

Today is Pat's birthday. I got her a ruby ring. It is supposed to have two tiny diamonds with it, but they may not be. Who knows? 8-1-81

I have tons of stuff to do grading two sets of papers, working on lectures, taking care of some academic dean stuff, preparing for Tuesday night Bible study, making notes from two books read, working on my Telugu lessons, writing letters, and probably something else I have forgotten. 8-6-81

The church situation improved in Bangarapet in terms of worship for our kids. We did occasionally attend a Telugu language church in a neighboring town, but SIBS had an English language service in the evenings that we attended.

At this point in India, we began to look into the possibility of adopting a baby. A family near Bangarapet had twins and one would probably be given up for adoption. Pat was keener on the idea than I was. But in the end a lawyer told us that we should not adopt any children unless their parents were either dead or unknown. However, we did help that family with milk for the 'extra' twin. Later we got in touch with an orphanage. A baby eventually became available, but Pat had just returned to the States with an undiagnosed illness (more on that later), so we did not adopt.

Jason said last night that the Lord told him he would be a missionary. He has always said before that he did not want to be a missionary, so this is a change. I know some men who felt (or thought they felt) the call of God as a child but did not follow through. But if God spoke to the boy Samuel, he can speak to Jason. Only time will tell. Kari said earlier that she would stay home [in the States] and preach. She would take care of us when we got old (50 or 60!). 8-21-81

As a professor at SIBS, I was also invited to preach at various meetings in Tanjore and Hyderabad. I also preached once at a Church of South India where I had my first experience of administering the cup during Communion. I did not know any of the standard affirmations that could be made at that point, so I served in silence. The priest and the people were not impressed.

In January of 1982, Pat began to have some abdominal pain. On the 30th, she had both of her cystic ovaries removed. This was the beginning of months of feeling bad, getting better, and hurting again. She had a second surgery on March 11 to remove a cystic mass. The doctors thought her problem might be related to the estrogen hormone that she had been taking for some years.

Before getting too far ahead, I must note that with Pat being out of commission, some of the kid's home schooling fell to me. Not good for them! The high point of those months was Jason's baptism on March 1 of 1982. This was an English language congregation in Bangalore.

Back to Pat. Her pain continued to go and come. Finally, she was encouraged by the doctors to return to the States where she could possibly get a diagnosis that was unobtainable in Bangalore.

Pat flew back to the States on May 1, 1982. The kids began to really miss her within a couple of weeks. I noted on the 12th that Jason had asked about her twice and that Kari had cried the night before.

My journal of that time is full of anxiety and prayers for Pat's safety and full recovery. Communication to the States was difficult, so I rarely heard her voice in those dark weeks.

I continued my habit of morning devotions and on June 6 I read from Philippians 4 and wrote, *I had forgotten verse 6; in my anxiety I have not thanked God for obvious blessings, e.g., the life of Pat, the health of my children, etc.* 6-6-82

That short entry hides the fact that this was something of a turning point in my spiritual life. Prior to that day, my prayer life had pretty much consisted of begging God to heal Pat. It was darkly colored with fear and despair. But that morning, I began again to thank God for his many, many blessings—without, of course, neglecting to intercede for Pat. But I had a peace that was almost tangible.

[In my suffering] *I have found a measure of peace and joy in thanksgiving. God has been so good to me in these past 14 years. I think few people have known the kind of love and unity Pat and I have shared and continue to share.* 6-8-82

I talked with Pat the next day and learned that the doctor had recommended that she stay in the States for a while. So, we began making arrangements to join her. I was thrilled.

From India to Callaway Gardens to Bangkok, Thailand

We had a snafu in the airport at Delhi as we tried to enter the terminal to catch our flight. I did not have Kari's or Jason's residential permit papers. The man behind the desk said I could not take them out of the country! He noted that he had know way of knowing if I was trying to take the children away from their mother. Finally, after some pleading (and tears from Kari) his supervisor said that we could go.

Reunited with a vibrant and healthy Pat, life was good again!

Eventually we went to Callaway Gardens in September to begin serving as missionaries-in-residence for the missionary orientation program of the Foreign Mission Board. It was good to be back in that beautiful place.

Kari and Jason have both gotten sweethearts. It is cute to see Jason and his girlfriend, but it is also sobering. They do grow up quickly. That sounds trite, but even though, it is true. 1-17-83

As visa requirements changed so that we were no longer able to return to India, we began to look at other possible assignments including Japan, Columbia, Peru, South Korea, East Indonesia, Finland, and Spain.

Soon, Thailand was added to the list. The final debate was between a teaching position in Cali, Columbia and a non-academic position in Thailand. Although I preferred to be teaching, my heart was still in Asia, so Thailand won the battle.

After orientation was over, I began to have some tingling in my right arm. The end result was surgery for a deteriorating disc in my neck. All went well.

We left for Thailand in early July of 1983.

Pat and I and the kids went to the stamp exhibition. We had a good time buying stamps. Today Kari went to Siam Park with the Pritchetts. The rest of us went to the new Central [Department Store] *and to the Weekend Market. We bought a kitten. I named her Princess Diana; Didi for short.* 8-6-83

Continuing his frightening ability to get hurt practically after every move we made, *Last night was rather hectic. Jason ran through a plate glass window at the Best's apartment building. We had to take him to the hospital where they put him to sleep and sewed him up. He came home this morning and is doing well. The cuts were superficial. One minor tendon in his left foot was partially severed, but the doctor sewed it up and put his foot in a cast.* 9-24-83

An outline of our first three years in Thailand:

1. We spent many months in language school. We were able to pass [barely!] a government exam that was a requirement of the school.

2. We made several good friends: Clif & Jeanne Best (with whom we stayed when we were flooded out of our house), Marku & Saya (missionaries from Finland who introduced us to the experience of the sauna), Ross & Bronwyn (missionaries from Australia), Chuck & Jenny Garcia (new FMB missionaries), Mark Sandlin (a journeyman missionary), Jack & Lynn Kinnison (FMB missionaries), and another FMBer, Jerry Perrill with whom I played many games of chess—losing more than I won.

3. We had a wonderful maid from northern Thailand. Her name was Surong. Later we would employ a couple of her sisters.

4. We were assigned to attend and work at Canaan Baptist Church during our first term. I was able to preach and teach some there.

5. We discovered the wonders of the Cameron Highlands for vacations.

6. I began to work in leadership training that was the position I had been brought in to fill. It included teaching with Jack Kinnison and Doug Ringer in northeastern Thailand at a leadership training school.

Now a few quotes and notes to fill in the spaces:

I went to the Tea Corner and talked to the cute waitress in Thai. Pat joined me after getting her hair done. The waitress brought another waiter over who wanted to become a Christian. We will bring Ajarn Samorn [pastor at Canaan] *with us there on Tuesday or Wednesday.* 2-18-24 This was the beginning of our witnessing with Taan, the waitress over a period of several months during which she became a language tutor for me and visited with us once in Pattaya. Unfortunately, none of this brought her to Christ—at least while we knew her.

From a holiday at the Baptist Camp in Pattaya: *I played golf Friday morning. Saturday Jason had a wreck riding a parachute behind a boat. He wasn't hurt bad. We should not have let him go. I just thank God he is okay. We played bridge, Trivial Pursuit, and chess* [with other missionaries] *I am reading a Ludlum book. . . . I also wrote four letters yesterday and worked on my stamps a little.* 12-3-84

I coached Jason's tee-ball team.

In early 1985, I began working at Christian Education while Bob Cullen was on furlough. At the same time, I also took over some of his responsibilities at the camp in Pattaya.

I was driving the car sometime this afternoon and I was possessed with doubts about Christianity. This is not the first time—and probably will not be the last. However, these periods of doubt are always fleeting. By God's grace, I will believe, doubts or no. 4-4-85 I can still remember the street scene on Sukhumvit the day it happened. It was perhaps a more significant event than this little reference seems to imply.

In May of 1985, I had my first leadership training meeting in Loei. Jack and Doug were the main leaders among us missionaries. Over the years, my responsibilities in Loei were some of my most rewarding work.

Although I was technically a leadership trainer working with church planters, I often disagreed with them. For example, I thought that starting small churches from small churches only produced weak, small churches. What we needed, I believed, was several big churches with small cell groups.

While in the Highlands again, I wrote, *we went to the Anglican Church today. I enjoyed the service. This afternoon I read Guyon's "Union with God". I need to wait on the Lord more in prayer. I need to listen. I also spent some time copying some hymn lyrics out of the hymn book I borrowed from the church. I want to incorporate them into my book of devotions.* 7-21-85

I should note that worshipping at this Anglican Church over the years was very meaningful to me in receiving Communion and participating in its beautiful liturgy. The 'book of devotions' is a book of quotes that were meaningful to me in a spiritual sense. I worked on it for several years but did not follow up very much after those first years.

Still in the Highlands, *we played our last round of golf here for this vacation. Today is Pat's birthday. Jason bought her a nice gift with his own money. Kari made her a pretty cross-stitch picture.* 8-1-85

I had a good meeting with [The] *Executive Committee this afternoon. I will find out tomorrow about teaching at the seminary. But whatever the decision is, I feel more at peace concerning my job here than in recent weeks. I attribute this to the prayers of several people—including Pat. I love her so very much!* 9-26-85

The next day I was given permission to teach one course at the seminary.

At a communication seminar, all the missionaries took the Myers-Brigg Inventory. I was (and) am an INFJ. Pat an ESFP. (For some reason, we later believed Pat was more of an N than an S.)

In November of 1985, Pat and I did a Marriage Encounter program. I really enjoyed it. We worked a bit with the organization for a while—having meetings in our house and helping with later programs.

Read Song of Solomon 1:1-4. Verse 3 is the bride's praise of her lover, but it reminded me also of Jesus. His 'oils have a pleasing fragrance'. His blessings make my heart rejoice. He has blessed me more than I could count. He has blessed me with Pat, my love. He has blessed me with children, friends, health, work, etc. And he gives me spiritual blessings like peace and joy. And occasionally moments of incredible sweetness. Perhaps others would call it emotional, not spiritual, but it is emotion imbued with peace—I take it to be from the LORD. . ... But greater than His oil is His Name which 'is like purified oil'. His blessings are pretty, as it were; but His Name is beautiful. He is beautiful; He is Perfection. His character, He-in-Himself is desirable above all others. The phrase 'purified oil' literally means 'oil which is emptied'. Paul tells us that He emptied Himself for my redemption. I praise and honor the name of my LORD Jesus Christ. 12-16-85

One of my more important contributions to the work was the development of a course on how to interpret the Bible. I taught this first at a church in Bangkok and later taught it at several other places.

I also wrote Sunday School lessons for Christian Education. These were used in Thailand and in the Philippines.

One final note: A proposal to increase mission meeting for one year had been rejected the year previous, but this next year (1986) it was approved. The extra day at the beginning was for the purpose of prayer and spiritual preparation. I had high hopes that it would make a difference. Alas, it did not. The mission remained divided over a number of issues.

Our First Furlough (1986-87)

Our furlough was around six months—mid July to early January. We furloughed in the missionary house provided by Dawson Memorial Baptist Church in Birmingham. We were active preaching and sharing about missions in other churches, but we did enjoy the times we were able to be in our Sunday School Class. When we were with them near Christmas time, they gave us some Christmas ornaments—several of which we continue to use.

Short notes:

1. I noted concerns about the Fundamentalists taking over so many of the Boards of SBC entities.

2. I enjoyed playing golf with some of the church members.

3. Kari, Jason and I went to a concert at Oak Mountain and saw The Bangles and Mr. Mister.

4. Jason played football.

5. I was still writing Sunday School lessons for Baptist Education in Thailand.

6. We visited New Orleans in October and discovered that Fisher Humphreys was struggling with a Fundamentalist board member at New Orleans Baptist Seminary.

7. We bought our first computer! It was in October of 1986.

8. Two movies that we saw in December were Golden Child (twice) and Star Trek IV.

Back in Thailand

Our return to Thailand was a drastic change from our first term there. Pat and I moved to Pattaya to work with Jack and Glad Martin in planting a church. I was also given responsibility for leadership training in the churches of the southern station. Kari and Jason stayed in the Baptist student hostel in Bangkok and continued their education at the fine International School there.

I noted on January 14, 1987 that *we needed to set some things straight with the Ollises about Jason. They may be overly strict.* Truth be told there was not much we could do. They were the dorm parents and in complete control—with parents having little influence in how their children were managed. This situation lasted for a whole year.

There was a Baptist church in the neighboring town of Banglamung that the Martin's and us attended regularly. But our main goal was to start a new church in Pattaya. My love for golf and some contacts that Jack had made (hotel owners who also played golf) payed off. I met an Australian man who played golf with me and the two hotel owners. He introduced us to his Filipino wife and her sister. Eventually they became part of our English language service in Pattaya.

We had two strategies for beginning two services: one in Thai and one in English. We spent a lot of time passing out tracts in downtown Pattaya—especially along the strip which bordered the ocean. The other was to offer English language classes at a center that we would open.

In April, we opened the Center which would serve as a place to teach English and have our worship services.

Short notes:

1. Surong's younger sister, Glin, became our maid.

2. On May 17, we baptized 5 persons in the ocean—one was for our church in Pattaya.

3. Jason and Kari stayed the summer with us. We dreaded their return to Bangkok.

4. I began to teach a course at the seminary in Bangkok, driving in two days a week.

5. I continued to travel in among the southern churches doing leadership training.

This has been a very busy week. And I am not at the end. Tuesday I taught English, studied [Thai] with khru, and prepared Bible lessons. Wednesday night I taught at Rayong and Thursday in Bangkok. We had a good visit with our kids. Jason asked us to move back in. I pray that Ex Com will approve it. 10-13-87

Eventually, they did approve our moving back which happened in January of 1988.

My workload increased in these next few years, though I never complained. I mostly enjoyed the work. I taught upcountry in several stations, at the seminary, at New Vision Baptist Church in Bangkok, and at the Baptist Student Center in Bangkok. I wrote commentary material for the Thai Study Bible that was being prepared by the Thailand Bible Society. I worked on material for the Song of Solomon, 2nd Peter, and Jude. I also continued to write Sunday School material for Christian Education. Lastly, I became Academic Dean of the seminary.

Four sad events occurred in those years. First, we got word of Eric's car wreck that left him quadriplegic. *This has been terrible shock and very depressing for us all. We called Pat's folks last night. I am concerned for all the family members now as well as for Eric. How will they react? Will they and he find peace and purpose in God? Help them Lord not to lose their faith. Hold them close."* 8-29-88

The second was Pat's four long months of suffering with back pain before she had successful back surgery in February 1989.

The third event occurred in June of 1989. We received the news that the Chinese military had slaughtered hundreds of demonstrators in the Tiananmen Square massacre. I was moved to tears reading about it in the Bangkok Post.

Not on par with those events in terms of seriousness was Kari returning *to* the States to begin college. *Kari left yesterday. It was a sad day. Jason even cried. He really misses her already. We all do.* 6-17-89

I remember some weeks later when Kari had a car wreck but wasn't hurt very much. That one night, I too cried.

The fourth one was the continued increase in the Fundamentalist takeover of the Southern Baptist Convention. In that year's annual meeting, the Convention passed a resolution that made the authority of the pastor more important than the priesthood of the believer. A few days after this, I wrote a letter in response in which I opposed the action. It was published in the Alabama Baptist.

Paige Patterson, whom I had met when he visited the work in Thailand, wrote me a rather condescending letter questioning what I had done. I replied in what I hoped was a Christian manner, but never heard from him again.

As always our life also had fun, light non-work-related moments. We enjoyed vacations in the Cameron Highland of Malaysia. I coached Jason's baseball team two years. The last year we were undefeated, and our all-star team won the southeastern Asia tournament. And Pat became a Catholic nun!!!! That is, she played a nun in a Thai movie. Yes, she was a movie star in Thailand 😊 I never saw the movie but talked with others who had seen it.

First Months Back in the States

This time we stayed in the mission house of McElwain Baptist Church. We did not get as close to anyone there as we had at Dawson. I would occasionally go down to the St. Luke's Episcopal church services that were held earlier.

We spent a lot of time doing deputation in churches, working in children's camps, being in World Mission Conferences wide and far. I was in one in California and another in Detroit!

All this time we were struggling with whether we could or should return to Thailand. I began to look at other possible places of ministry in the States.

I wrote several letters to state conventions yesterday. I pray that God will give us wisdom in deciding our future plans. At this point in my life, I look back and am pleased with where I have been. While I am not entirely satisfied with all that I have done in those places, I do not feel that at any point God was displeased with my being there. May the future reflect the past? 9-20-91

We visited with old friends. This included Philip and Cynthia Wise. Philip mentioned a church in Buffalo that he thought might be a good fit for us.

On October the Board of the FMB decided to defund Ruschlikon seminary in Switzerland because Glenn Hinson (a bane of Fundamentalists) had taught there on Sabbatical for four months.

Most of yesterday I was touched with depression. The decision of the FMB to cut off Ruschlikon . . . has begun to eat away at me. Unless they reverse their decision in December, I don't see how I can go back to Thailand. Part of my concern was that with me at the seminary in Thailand, the Fundamentalist might target it.

With our resignation looking more and more likely, I began to seek other positions of ministry. I got in touch with churches from Detroit to Milwaukee to Birmingham. I also checked in on Samford and Mobile College. I actually interviewed for a position at Judson College (an all-women's Baptist college in south Alabama), but did not get a call.

I had great support from my Trinity Group friends. We were meeting twice a year at that time to talk mostly about theology and the problems in the SBC.

One thing I enjoyed was taking a writing course from Writer's Digest School. I actually wrote some futuristic fiction short stories. I sent at least one of them to several magazines, but it was never published.

The Board of the FMB met again in December and refused to reverse their decision about defunding the seminary in Switzerland. So, we decided to resign though we did not send our resignation letter in until March. We continued to fulfill responsibilities of speaking on missions at various events.

I wrote a prayer after reading Psalm 9, *O LORD You are a stronghold in times of trouble. You are ever mindful of the afflicted. May my life reflect Your character? Help my LORD to be tenderhearted to those who suffer. Help me to be a guide leading others to the Stronghold. I thank You LORD for the many joys of my life; for Pat, Kari, and Jason; for friends; for opportunities to teach and preach; for worship and prayer; for health; for recreation. Although I was unworthy, you loved me and through Jesus You saved me. And You love me still. Your Spirit is with me. Literally forever I am in Your debt, but it is a debt of joy and not a burden. Bless my children, LORD. May they know the joy of Your salvation forever.* 3-11-92

One wonderful event in our family during this time was the marriage of Kari and Patrick on April 10, 1992. It was a beautiful wedding. We were glad to welcome Patrick into our family.

In June we traveled to Buffalo to meet the pastor search committee and the church.

Yesterday Tom and Nora took us downtown and then to Niagara Falls. It was an enjoyable time. In the afternoon we met with the DOM [Director of Missions] and the church start strategist. It was not so enjoyable. They are typical HMB [Home Mission Board, later North American Mission Board] fundamentalists and/or bureaucrats. Last night we had supper with the Merediths and the search committee and spouses. . .. The Merediths are clearly moderates. We mesh well. 6-7-92 The last sentence turned out to be wrong.

Pat and I had a good talk yesterday evening. I feel better about going to Buffalo. I was afraid of a lot of things. Like getting lost in a 40-member church for the next 5 – 10 years without any good prospects. I was disappointed by the inherent lack of moving toward a more liturgical service. I have been attracted to Anglican-Episcopal worship for years. I am presently reading" Evangelicals on the Canterbury Trail." It has increased those longings. But for now, I will worship God in my Baptist tradition. There is much that is good about it as well. 6-14-92

I worshipped at St. Luke's this morning. For the first time as I watched the line of people approaching the altar, I was struck by the reality that I was participating today with millions of others in the same response to the gospel, e.g., receiving the sacrament with faith and thanksgiving. It gives me a sense of the corporate Body of Christ and being part of it. 6-28-92

University Baptist Church in Getzville, New York

In some ways, this is the hardest section to write. While here there were good experiences and new friends, the work at the church was depressing. However, it is all part of my remembered story and part of what makes me who I am today. The church was 'progressive' in terms of the controversy in the Southern Baptist Convention at that time. They were solidly with the Cooperative Baptist Fellowship. It seemed like a good fit.

My first sermon at UBC was "On Loving God with our Minds". Our first purchase was Gretchen, a half Rottweiler, half German Shepherd puppy.

Yesterday morning Pat and I met with the [Christian Ministerial Association executive committee] to be approved as campus ministers at the State University of New York, Buffalo. Afterward we went into Buffalo where Pat applied for a Head Start job. Bill Bauza and I went to the Jazz Festival at Artpark from 3 to 5:30 and 8:30 to 11:30. In between we returned to UBC for First Friday [a gathering of church members and friends and college students which was held once a month]. 9-5-92

The church had applied for funds from the Home Mission Board to help with my salary. They had received it before, but this time it was denied.

Jason, Kari, and Patrick joined us for that first Christmas in Buffalo. We had a good time together. We made a trip to the Canadian side of Niagara Falls. It was beautiful. I think it was perhaps the next month when Pat and I returned there to find the Falls almost completely frozen over. It was a breathtaking sight with the trees sparkling with drops of frozen mist from the Falls.

In 1993, I began a Bible study with mostly women from Sri Lanka. We had the study in the home of one of our members, Christine Vijaykumar. These meetings were wonderful!

Another event in 1993 was the opportunity I had to serve as a chaplain at the World University Games which were held in Buffalo that year.

My journals were colored with depressing realities: *"I am concerned about our future. We lose Tom next week. The Kims will be leaving in a very few months. Visitors came but do not return. When school is out, we will be losing Modisa and his family. The Hwangs and MacKenzies have dropped out. ... We need some new members just to stay even and staying even won't pay the bills in future years. ... Draw people into our church LORD that we might be more effective in our worship and service. Help us to be pleasing to you. Give me wisdom and insight that I might be pleasing to You as pastor of your people. Help me—help us. Without You, we are lost.* 3-22-93

Again, there were positives. I wrote devotionals for Smyth & Helwys' "Reflections". I began teaching at Southern Seminary's extension program in Pittsburgh. I taught some courses at the University. The first was on mysticism in world religions.

I baptized Larry Prince, who until his death a year to so later, was a wonderful member. We met the Idol family who eventually joined the church and became good friends. And I was always with Pat! *Yesterday I . . . ate lunch with Pat. I got her a nice flower arrangement. I inscribed it 'Heaven lasts forever, and it began 25 years ago'.* 8-3-93

It is a beautiful day with the sun shining out of a blue sky onto the snow-covered ground. Wisps of white clouds could almost be reflections of the white earth. Saturday afternoon Pat and I visited the Konovitz family. They came to church on Sunday. [They were a rather poor family who eventually joined the church and became pretty regular worshippers.] In the late afternoon and early evening 10 of us from BCM [Baptist Campus Ministries] took in the Festival of Lights in Niagara Falls. It was COLD, but fun . . . Pat and I went to see 'Les Miserables' Sunday afternoon. We thoroughly enjoyed it, in spite of being in the next to last row of the upper balcony. That was our Christmas gift to each other. 12-13-93

My first sermon of 1994 was on the lessons we should have learned from the Hippies, i.e., things are not important, but community and peace are.

Financially we continued to struggle. I received $400 a month as Baptist Campus Minister, which enabled UBC to reduce our salary by that much. Pat was working at a Day Care Center. Through that job we met Gretchen and David Difante and their daughter Lauren. They were Methodists and not interested in moving churches, but they became some of our best friends there.

I noted in March that the Merediths (and perhaps others) were becoming disgruntled with me. The Merediths were one of the founding families of the church. Dale (the husband) was the Moderator of the church. We had no deacons.

As our struggles continued at the church we began to look at other opportunities. We even considered returning to Thailand, but communication with people at the Board indicated that we would not be reappointed by the FMB. In the next few months and into 1995, I applied for several teaching positions, but none of them materialized.

Pat began working on a master's in special education at Buffalo State College—a degree that promised her years of good work in a field that she enjoyed.

By June of '94, attendance had fallen so low on Wednesday nights that we discontinued that Bible study.

A nearby housing development had a child-care center that used our education building on rainy days. The development was called Audubon. They had an ordinance that did now allow peddlers (including peddlers of the gospel) to go door to door. However, I was able to make flyers that I could insert into the boxes of the children at the daycare center where their parents would receive them. This and other programs that I attempted never brought in new members. I did baptize a few persons and others joined by letter, but the future continued to look bleak.

July 21-23 was a pivotal three days in my life. I attended a Gathering of Baptists Interested in Spirituality. It was held at Mars Hill College in North Carolina. (Later the name was changed to Baptists <u>and Others</u>.) Glen Hinson, the pre-eminent expert on spirituality among Baptists in the South, was the primary speaker. I met some new friends and contacts. (One would lead to a writing assignment with Smyth & Helwys. Another, years later, would lead a series of retreats at different monasteries that I attended on numerous occasions.) This became a meeting that I would attend either once or twice every year I was in the States until it was finally discontinued. But in those several years, it was the source of a spiritual vitality that I needed. This first meeting spurred me to provide more opportunities for spiritual formation at UBC. (This too was not very well received.)

After church last night, Dale told me that the 12-week running average was the lowest it had been since 1991. The last 6 weeks or so have been abysmal in terms of attendance. Summertime is always low, but this year it has been much more so. Why? Is it just a fluke or does it reflect a more serious problem? 9-11-94

One rather unique experience occurred at the University. A couple of Wiccan students took my mysticism class one semester. During that semester I was invited to speak at one of their meetings on Christian mysticism. I spoke on the mystical life as seen in Jesus Christ. It seemed well-received.

On November 23, I noted that Jason and "a new friend, Lori Adams" had come up for the weekend!

In December, Pat got a graduate assistant's position at her college. I told her that I had prayed that she would get it—unless someone needed it more. Her reply as that it must mean we are pretty needy! So, starting then, Pat would work at Rich's Day Care in the daytime, go to school at night, and do the graduate assistant's job somewhere in all of that.

Last night I was asked to give the invocation and benediction at the annual Martin Luther King, Jr. address [sponsored by the University]. Harry Belafonte was the keynote speaker. He spoke with passion and eloquence. He spoke for well over an hour without any notes. He spoke of his own personal history, of the civil rights movement, of how black leaders are now part of the system, of how his own dream of an end to racism was largely unfulfilled, of how the political turn in the country [Ronald Reagan years] is a catastrophe but may mobilize us again to fight. He had little good to say about God or religion and in that I think he is missing the mark, but the rest was wonderful. 2-24-95

In 1995, I began writing Sunday School lessons for Smyth & Helwys. It was also in that year when I was contracted by Smyth & Helwys to write *Growing Spiritually with Saints: Catherine of Genoa and William Law.*

On June 13, I noted that the Sunday night business meeting had been fraught with conflict. The details don't matter, but I did note that Dale and Jean didn't want to pursue sources for getting funds to help support the pastor (me). The idols were mortified. I think it was the first time I wrote that we were going to leave by the first of the year—though our options were pretty limited.

I also wrote later that in a visit with Satish and Usha Mohindra (faithful members of the church) that they said they were looking for another church. They had become increasingly upset over the authoritarian hold one or two families had over the church. It encouraged me to think that some of those who had left the church during my time there had perhaps left because of that circumstance instead of me.

Jason and Lori left early this morning. We had a good time visiting coffee shops, bookstores, restaurants, and movie houses. They did a good job with the testimony Sunday morning. Kari called to tell us that she is expecting. She is ecstatic. . .. Needless to say, Pat and I are excited. 9-9-95

I have mentioned Bill Bauza once or twice. He was the music director. His wife, Marg, was the pianist. They had become upset over the Meredith's reading during my sermons!

A friend from the Trinity Group and pastor of Vestavia Hills Baptist Church, Gary Furr and his daughter Heather, came to visit and lead a retreat for the church. Some 20 folks attended.

Gary and I had a meal just before they left. He looked me in the eye and said that the situation at UBC was not my fault. It certainly made me feel better.

As we continued to think about leaving the first of the year, three positions were possible. One was a Baptist Campus Minister at Columbia in New York City. Someone else got that one. The other two were pastorate in Madison, Alabama and a teaching position at New Orleans Theological Baptist Seminary.

Sunday was a turning point day. I did announce my resignation [effective after December 17]. There were shock and tears. I was wavering until just before church when I talked with Pat again. Sue Tubbs was out sick, so I don't know how she will respond, but I believe she will be supportive. Both Pat and I were surprised with how upset Marg was. We didn't think she cared that much. We did have an inkling when Brenda told us Thursday that Marg had talked to her about speaking to Jean to the effect that if they didn't change their open attitude toward me, she would not do a Christmas program! She and Bill have been incensed that the Merediths read during my sermons! Now we wait for calls from NOBTS and/or Madison. And we pray that God will guide the future. 11-27-95

We actually got a call from Madison before NOBTS offered us a position. But I was somewhat fearful of taking another pastorate. So, shortly afterwards we got a call from the seminary offering me an untenured position teaching missions and theology. All of our friends at UBC were relieved that we had somewhere to go after leaving Buffalo.

Pat and I stayed busy with packing and related chores. . ... Sunday we had the biggest one-day snowstorm in Buffalo history—over three feet. 12-11-95

New Orleans Baptist Seminary

That snowstorm came in behind us as we left Buffalo, but we made it South without any problems. We arrived in New Orleans on January 1, 1996.

Our old friends Gerald and Kathy Wright put us up for a couple of nights before our town house was ready.

When we moved in we met our new neighbors, Darryl and Mary Catherine Ferrington and their 2 sons and 1 daughter. They were good neighbors and friends.

In addition to Gerald, I was also able to reconnect with Fisher Humphreys at the seminary and a childhood buddy, Ben Alford who was pastoring an Episcopal church in New Orleans.

I loved New Orleans—the French Quarter, the music scene, Mardi Gras, golf, etc. On March 7, Darryl and I went to the House of Blues and heard Alison Krauss and Union Station. It would not be my last trip there.

Pat and I *had a full weekend. Saturday we went to the Jazz Brunch at The Court of Two Sisters. The food was fabulous. The atmosphere was conducive to a leisurely morning of talking. The music was nice. After sitting down at the Riverwalk overlooking the Mississippi, we went to the aquarium which I enjoyed. . .. Then we went to the Riverwalk Mall where Pat and I bought hats. [Afterwards] we rode the streetcar back to Carrolton where we had parked the car.* 3-19-96

I probably should mention that I had gone to New Orleans on a one-year contract. A new president was coming in and they did not want to hire me at that time as a regular professor.

In April, I was called to Vieux Carre Baptist Church as their interim pastor. It was small church in the French Quarter. I had great hopes of helping the church become more appropriate to their French Quarter setting. Although I was called "interim", the church was not financially able to call a full-time pastor, so I could stay as long as I wanted to.

Caitlyn Alyssa Harris was born on Tuesday at 6:14pm. 5-9-96

I really enjoyed my time in the French Quarter as part of my connection to Vieux Carre Baptist Church. Coffee houses and pastry shops abound! I even walked up and down all the streets and made a map of the various roads and the businesses on each of them. Just getting to know the neighborhood ☺

An event happened that soured the joy we were feeling. Pat's mom, Mildred, had a malignant tumor removed from one of her lungs. The next couple of years were especially hard on Pat.

We had a good visit with Kari, Patrick, and Caitlyn. Caitlyn is beautiful. I pray that she will grow in the beauty of godliness. We rode the streetcar and saw a couple of movies. Patrick and I played golf a couple of times. . .. They left before church. We had a good service. One young black homeless male came forward to give his life to Christ. His name is Adrian. 7-8-96

The Division of Theology and Church History strongly recommended that I be hired in the permanent position to teach theology and missions. However, the new President was part of the Fundamentalist movement within the Southern Baptist Convention. That year I had had my first book published; *Growing Spiritually with the Saints: Catherine of Genoa and William Law.* It was published by Smyth & Helwys, a Baptist publishing house associated with the moderate movement of the Cooperative Baptist Fellowship. I was also good friends with Fisher Humphreys, the professor that Fundamentalist trustees wanted gone. I heard too that the president of the FMB did not recommend me.

So, it was not a total surprise, when I found out that *Dr. Kelley has decided not to offer me a permanent position. Pat is hurting, the division is upset, and I am certainly disappointed. I don't think that I am as upset or hurt or crushed as some had feared. Being an InfJ [Myers-Brigg profile] I'm not sure what my feelings are, but I am confident that other opportunities of service and ministry will be forthcoming.* 8-26-96

Dr. Kelley did give me an additional term to teach, so I continued to teach for another two terms, and I continued to serve at Vieux Carre. Pat had a job she loved. She was working at an inclusive daycare center in the Garden District of New Orleans. Because of her love for that job and my love for New Orleans, I hoped to find a ministry position of some kind in New Orleans.

So, for several months I searched for ministry jobs in New Orleans. I talked with the Episcopal bishop in New Orleans and the Methodist supervisor. I contacted Loyola's religious department. I also looked beyond New Orleans at various teaching positions. Eventually I decided not to move to the Episcopal or Methodist churches. The Episcopal bishop was going to require an additional year of education for me in Tennessee—which we could not afford. And the Methodist supervisor was looking at a church in Baton Rouge for my first assignment.

However, two positives came from these months of searching. First, was the taking of a unit of Clinical Pastoral Education to consider hospital chaplaincy as a career change. The unit of study was wonderful, but in the end I decided that the chaplaincy was not for me.

The second was the Episcopal bishop suggesting that I start doing spiritual direction with a priest named Steve Halzhalb to help me in the discernment process. Steve encouraged me to use the Book of Common Prayer which I have done regularly for the past 20+ years. He also encouraged me to attend to the spiritual practices of silence and using a breath prayer. My meetings with him really were life changing.

On Sunday I announced to the staff that I would be resigning as interim pastor. December 15 will be my last Sunday. Pat and I may go to St George's [where Ben Alford was the Episcopal priest]. Pat is seeing Asa for some counseling. She is hurting related to her mom's condition and to my uncertain vocational future. I pray that God will bless her through him. 11-4-96

In early 1997, I was contacted by First Baptist Church of Montezuma, Georgia. My work with Steve, had helped me to overcome my fear of pastoring again, so I was willing to consider that move.

In early March, I preached for the pastor search committee. They came to Mt. Calvary Baptist Church in Albertville to hear me. We had a good time meeting with them. They recommended me to the church and later sent us a financial package to consider.

Even at that point, I was still hoping something would materialize in New Orleans. *I am meeting with the pastor of St. Charles Avenue Baptist Church at 11. I want to talk with him about job opportunities. Tomorrow I will talk with Jennie about what it means to become a Presbyterian. . .. Pat will probably be offered the directorship [of the childcare center where she was working], so we will stay in New Orleans if I can find adequate employment. Montezuma is the other option. May God led us. Give us wisdom.* 4-28-97

May brought 3 good changes into our lives. First, and least significant ☺, I bought a 1991 red Miata rag-top convertible. I loved that car! Second, we visited Montezuma and had a good time with the pastor search committee. I loved the stained-glass windows of the church. Third, Jason and Lori were married on the 25th in a beautiful, multi-ethnic ceremony in Birmingham.

This past weekend we went to Montezuma where I preached in view of a call. The vote was 135 to 16. A couple of hardnosed Fundamentalists are there, but they will leave or sit on the back benches. I am not worried about them. 6-3-97 Their main issue seemed to be my willingness to accept some abortions. I did note later that two of those families apologized for opposing my coming and they affirmed my pastorate there.

First Baptist Church, Montezuma, Georgia

In the first two weeks, there were 3 deaths in 8 days! I also had to endure a July 4 Sunday service that had more patriotic stuff than I was comfortable with. But overall, it was a good beginning. Pat and I visited shut ins. We attended fun youth functions—one at which we played nertz. I played golf at the little nine-hole course in Montezuma. I joined the Kiwanis Club. Preston (chairman of the deacons and mayor of the town) and Sarah Williams arranged a dinner at which we met Kirby Godsey, the president of Mercer University.

Shortly afterwards Pat went to be with her mother who was not doing well. Mildred died a short while later. I did her funeral as she had requested. A funny thing happened earlier. When she asked if I would preach at her funeral, I said that I would be glad to!!! Of course, what I meant was that I would be glad to honor her wishes. Everyone laughed, including Mildred.

Thursday, I had breakfast [at Grover's Grits] with Chip and Eric [local Methodist and Lutheran pastors]. We had a good visit. In the evening, we ate with the Taylors [the husband was a deacon who produced home made wine]. Friday morning, I played golf with Tony [the youth director]. Saturday morning, we had a good Church Council meeting. Then in the evening, about a dozen youth came to our house to watch Buffy the Vampire Slayer. Sunday's attendance was down with about 10 of our men at a Promise Keepers meeting. But the morning Communion service was good. 10-6-97

In November of 1997, I began writing Sunday School lessons again for Smyth & Helwys. November was a good month at the church with several persons being baptized. We also got an inactive member back because I send him a birthday card. I started sending birthday cards to all the resident members of the church. It was a practice I continued in my later pastorates as well.

In December, I started going to an early Tuesday morning Communion service at the Episcopal Church in Americus. The pastor and I got to know each other. One year, he invited me to speak on a Wednesday night about my spiritual practices. And for Christmas that year, dad gave me $50 most of which I used to buy a small leather-bound Book of Common Prayer which was easier to carry around. I still use today—over 20 years later.

In April of 1998, my mom had heart surgery for blocked arteries. The surgery was successful, but her kidneys failed, and she died on the 20th. Although in a note we found that she had written some years before about her funeral wishes in which she stipulated that she wanted only one preacher to preach, Tom and I both preached. Tom laughed and said that the two of us probably made up one preacher. In my part, I talked about how mom was a person of prayer and how she taught me first to pray, "now I lay me down to sleep and pray the Lord my soul to keep and if I die before I wake, I pray the Lord my soul to take." Later she taught me to pray the Lord's Prayer.

In May I made a trip to New Orleans for Jazz Fest. I was able to go each year that we were in Montezuma. Also, in May, I started morning prayers at Montezuma on Mondays. Sharing the Lord's Supper was always part of those mornings. Attendance was sparse, but faithful. I loved doing it.

In that same month, I also noted that I had been asked to teach New Testament Introduction at Mercer University in Macon. This was the first of several opportunities I had to teach different courses there as an adjunct professor. I love doing that as well.

I am at mom's graveyard. It is Memorial Day weekend, so a lot of folks are milling around. I decided to do my devotions here. Mom encouraged me to pray as a kid so I think she is happy that I would pray here. I don't know if she knows what is going on. Perhaps she is too full of praise for God to notice. But since God pays attention to His creation, maybe she does as well. I am convinced that if she see it, she sees it from God's perspective and is filled with His bliss. She has no melancholy or sad moments and for that I am glad. 5-23-98

In 1998, the town formed a Council for Community Unity. Its purpose was to promote unity among the black and white population. I became the chairperson of the committee. We planned musical programs and Christmas parades that were designed to bring folks together. I don't know how effective we were, but I believed it was an important part of my ministry to the community.

In June we had a great visit with Jason and Lori in California. We went to Napa Valley; visited with student friends; went to bookstores, cd stores, gift and hippy-style stores; and had some great conversations.

I started a new Sunday School class for adults who were not attending one already. It was a hit. We had 10 or more to come almost every Sunday while we were there.

Caitlyn is a hoot around our new kitten, Sasha. She is scared of her; not such that she cries, but she sure wants to be held. Sometimes she gets almost brave enough to pet her, but then panic takes over. 6 18 98

I met with [two ladies from our church]. We talked about race and a Unity Council proposal to start a community wide youth choir. They have typical reservations about it as minority whites who lived through black rioting in the 70s. I have discovered in my own life how insidious racial prejudice is, so I have less distain for those who suffer with it. May God give me wisdom, patience, and love to be able to promote harmony. 7-16-98

We took the youth to New Orleans where they sang and gave testimonies in an open area of the French Quarter. We did some sight-seeing as well. It was a really good time. The only downer was that our youth director (Tony) told me that he and his wife were having problems. Eventually they divorced and moved away from Montezuma.

Pat continued to go with me sometimes to the Gathering of Baptists (and Others) Interested in Spirituality. She expressed feeling drawn to such spirituality.

In August of 1998, Pat and I began to take turns with Tom and Jackie in caring for dad. We would meet about halfway between Albertville and Montezuma to swap him back and forth. He mostly enjoyed being with his two different sons. He was much loved at the church in Montezuma. He loved to go to Grover's Grits!

The year is not ending well in terms of regular devotions! There are no excuses. I do not get up early enough on Tuesdays and Thursdays to do them before going to Macon [to teach]. I have allowed my work schedule to interfere on other days. Then over the Thanksgiving holidays, I just let it slip. Others think I am strong in the spiritual life of prayer. I know better! . . . I have three projects: 1) a study on 'righteousness' for tonight 2) lecture on the Book of Revelation [for Mercer], 3) prepare Sunday morning's sermon. That still leaves several other things left to do prepare for the ministers and spouses' retreat on Friday, prepare for Sunday School, prepare for Sunday night. But none of this work will be sufficient if I do not first prepare myself. Fill me Lord with your Spirit. How symbolic that I ran out of ink between 'your' and 'Spirit'. I need you. 12-2-98

For Christmas in 1998, my sweet Pat got me a Celtic cross, a statue of St. Francis, and an Espresso-Cappuccino machine! Did she know me or what?!!

Three events in February of 1999 that are worth noting. 1) Howard (our church music director) and his wife Debbie went with us to Atlanta to hear a folk concert. We had a good time. 2) We bought a chocolate lab puppy. We named it LaMon's Nubian Princess—Nubi for short. She was one of my favorite dogs. 3) I attended a Walk to Emmaus at which the highlight was Saturday night when after a session, the spiritual director said to get ready to see the face of Jesus. We walked out into the night and there lining the walkway were candles being held by a multitude of people. Those people, including some from Montezuma, were indeed the presence of Jesus to us.

I find it interesting looking at saints on whose feast day I was born. Salvatore of Horta, a Franciscan lay brother, of whom I know very little. May I not crave popularity or a name well-known. May I be faithful in following you, Lord God. Edward the Martyr, king of England. He did not die for the faith, and unless circumstances change drastically, neither will I. But help me Lord to die in the faith. Frigidian, perhaps an Irishman. . . .. And if, as some suppose, he is identical with Finnian of Moville, he was a lover of books. I appreciate the Celtic heritage. May I learn from it that which would help my life. Cyril of Jerusalem is certainly the most well-known. Like Cyril, help me Lord to be a faithful pastor to your flock. 3-18-99

On May 12, our next-door neighbor, Lynn Gresham was murdered outside his home. He was a local banker, a deacon in our church, and a good man. He was mourned and missed.

On the last Sunday in May I baptized 14 people, and 2 others three weeks before that.

In October, Tom and I sold mom and dad's old house. Pat and I used most of the money we got to pay off bills.

Jason and Lori stayed with us some in October before leaving for Indonesia. Our time with them reignited our interest in missions. We got some material from the Cooperative Baptist Fellowship, but nothing was available in Bali which has a majority Hindu population or in Thailand. I did write that *things are going well at First Baptist and I enjoy teaching at Mercer, so I am in no rush to move.* 11-19-99

I was listening to Indian chants by Ravi Shankar as I wrote in my journal. *It may be because the Indian chants are playing in the background, but this morning I miss the mission field. Pat and I would be interested in Thailand or Bali. . . . But thus far there is no opening with CBF. Lord if a way to serve you in those places or others of similar background is possible, open it. But I waver. Bless me with wisdom in my responsibilities to my dad and to Caitlyn.* 1-12-00

We have some little ragamuffins attending church and some folks are offended. According to Mrs. Janet [who brought them], some have even suggested that these kids might be more comfortable somewhere else. I don't know what it would take for some of our folks to welcome with open arms all who would seek Christ. . . . May God help me to preach and teach his Word in a clear and winsome way. 2-22-00

We talked about our future. Pat wants to be settled, preferably where she can relate to family and grandkids. She is very ambiguous—to put it mildly—about going back overseas. . . . That brings me to evaluate why I am willing to consider missions. 1) It means gong into a new and exciting situation. 2) It is a way to move from Montezuma—more on that in a moment. 3) With little or no prospects for teaching missions is a good way to finish my ministerial career. 4) We would return to Thailand or go to Bali. Either would be a return to mission roots and call. 5) We could promote the Good News among people who do not know it. 6) Simplified living with a stronger devotional life. . . . Now why am I interested in moving from Montezuma? All the reasons seem selfish. The future of the town is in doubt as whites die and/or move away. Which means, not that the town will die, but that First Baptist will be harder and harder to sustain. Fellowship strains are resurfacing which means added pressure on me. I find myself increasingly moved by feelings of antagonism to certain members—mostly the whiners and complainers. Racial bigotry and prejudice is ever present in some of the best of our church members. Definitely God has used who I am, my gifts and talents, to minister here. The question is, could who I am be more effectively used elsewhere? I believe so, but it may not happen. And if it doesn't, I believe God will protect my spirit. By his grace, I will not lose any desire to minister and serve God and his Kingdom here. I reread my thoughts and two more came to mind. One, I am disappointed that [very few] of the host who joined the church in 1999 have become regular in attendance or entered into the life of the congregation. Part of that must be my fault, but I don't know what to do. Two, am I suffering from another bout of mid-life crisis? I have only 15 years or so left in terms of pre-retirement age ministry. The end is staring me in the face. How do I want to spend my last years? What are my options? . . . May God help me to be faithful to him, to Pat, and to myself—in that order! 3-8-00

In late March or early April, I went to a preaching conference in Atlanta. While I was there, I ate a meal with a former missionary colleague, Graham Walker. He was in talks with the mission sending agency of the American Baptist Churches about how Mercer University could work with the Asia Graduate Baptist Theological Seminary. He though that they might be open to me teaching in Thailand with one of the schools connected to AGBTS. With the prospect of going back to Thailand, this time to Chiang Mai, Pat was quickly on board.

Our second grandchild was born on April 27—Jordan Aleksandr Harris. Needless to say, we all were happy and excited!

Things moved pretty quickly in May. We filled out forms for International Ministries of American Baptist Churches. The Asian leadership approved of our coming. This was important because IM of ABC gets approval from their indigenous partners before sending missionaries or starting new work. A visa slot opened up at Payap University in Chiang Mai with the unexpected departure of one of their missionary teachers. I also told the church in Montezuma what was happening, and while they hated to see us go, they were gung-ho in supporting us.

The SBC approved a new Baptist Faith & Message today. They deleted [articles on] soul competency and priesthood of the believer. They deleted reference to Christ as the criterion by which the Bible is to be interpreted. They affirmed that only men could be pastors. . ... It is a sad, sad day. I just hope that this will not negatively impact Jason and Lori. I fear for Paul Robertson's job [at New Orleans Baptist Seminary]. I just don't know how much more he can stand. 6-14-00

Because of the drastic changes in the SBC over the years, we felt good about becoming missionaries with International Ministries of American Baptist Churches. In the summer of 2000, we had our orientation and commissioning by IM of ABC. I was very impressed by their culture. American Baptists are the most racial diverse denomination in America. And they are very diverse on the theological spectrum. International Ministries is committed to working in tandem with national partners and IM practices 'high trust, low control' in terms of how they relate to their missionaries.

Before leaving for the field, we needed to join an American Baptist Church. We opted for Oakhurst Baptist Church in Decatur, Georgia. The church was also affiliated with the Alliance of Baptists and the Cooperative Baptist Fellowship. They were a welcoming and affirming church in terms of lesbians and gays. However, when we met with the deacons for approval of our membership application (for we had never worshipped in the church), they never asked us for our own opinions. In other words, being welcoming and affirming was not a requirement for membership. Over the years, as we worshipped in the church while on furlough, we learned to love them all. It is a great congregation.

Back in the Kingdom of Thailand

First Term in Chiang Mai

We arrived in Chiang Mai on September 23, 2000. We were met at the airport by representatives from the school and from the mission. Lisa and John Simmons were the missionaries charged with helping us settle in. They did a great job. John was also a golfer, so he introduced me to golfing in Chiang Mai.

When we arrived on campus, we were given an air-conditioned room in the student hostel—on the males' side. We were there for several weeks as we waited for our professor house to be readied for us to move in. We walked out on the street for lunch that first day and enjoyed some simple Thai food.

Today my life truly begins in Chiang Mai. I pray for God's blessings. As we go this morning for language study, I pray that we will learn new words and new phrases. May we gain greater understanding of Thai ways and thoughts. Then as I return to teach my first class, give me courage. Help me to speak with clarity and winsomeness. Help me to understand what is said to me. May I help the students this term to come to a greater understanding and appreciation for the Book of Psalms. And finally, today as I set up my office, may I not be overly sad for the books and things that are missing. [One or two boxes were lost in transit.] I am thankful that my dissertation, my book [Growing Spiritually with the Saints], and my favorite copy of "Theologia Germanica" made it. And I pray that Underhill may yet be found. Thank you Lord for the church service yesterday. I pray that Pat and I will make contributions to the life of the church. . ... Gracious and holy God let my thoughts turn often to you who are the beauty and glory of my life. Amen. 10-16-00

I taught at the McGilvary School of Divinity of Payap University. Payap was a school sponsored by the Church of Christ in Thailand—a union church composed of Presbyterian, American Baptist, and Disciples of Christ churches.

Very quickly after we arrived the missionary chaplain of the university, started a regular contemplative meeting at our chapel. It was mostly for English speaking ex-pats. I joined in with them for times of silence and meditations on readings. I was pleased to find this emphasis—though the meetings did not endure for long.

The contemplative 'service' took for me an unexpected turn last Friday night. After the first 30 minutes of Taize music we had begun silence. For about 15 minutes or so I worked on it. In connection with my breath prayer, 'Beautiful Lord, enflame my heart', I began to concentrate on beauty—God's beauty. After about 15 minutes, I was ready to stop but wanted to persevere for at least another 15 minutes. . . . Suddenly I found myself saying in my heart something like the following: 'Lord, beautiful Lord, how can I remain silent in the presence of your glorious beauty? Your beauty is more colorful than a rainbow, brighter than the sun, more intense than the orchids in bloom. How can I remain silent? All the beauty of the world is but a pale reflection of your eternal beauty. Only in the day when I see your face in all your Glory will I be unable to speak as I sit in rapt attention bathed in your perfect beauty. Till then may I praise you, most beautiful One.' It was a moving experience. Thank you, gracious Lord. 11-12-00

The quotation above reflects my own lack in the area of practicing silence. The mentors of this spiritual discipline normally recommend two periods a day of 20 minutes each sitting in silence with a quiet mind. They have recommendations on how to quiet one's mind and return to the silence. I know that there is value in silence; that it is a genuine spiritual discipline. Nevertheless, it has never 'worked' much for me though I have tried it at different times in my life—and still do today.

In mid-November, we attended our first Loi Kratong celebrations. While the smoke from fireworks and the noise from the crowds were not pleasant, I was impressed by the sky lit with fire-breathing balloons and the river sparkling with lines of floating candles.

In December, I did a personal walking tour of Chiang Mai. I saw some quiet peaceful Buddhist temples (called 'wats' in Thailand) where I knew I could come sometime and sit for my devotions. There were a few other temples that were more tourist friendly and thus not as peaceful.

I confess to my lack of commitment to daily devotions. I confess my unwillingness to regularly practice meditation, contemplation, and silence. I confess that my prayers of intercession have been perfunctory. Forgive me Lord and make me whole. Amen. This morning I had decided to read a letter or two of [Evelyn] Underhill's and let that 'count' as morning devotions. I could do that while eating breakfast and then check the news and emails. However, in the first paragraph she wrote, 'Where <u>had</u> your sense of proportion gotten to, when you thought you had not time for your morning prayers.' Ouch! As for intercession, she admonished her reader to use 'the whole strength of our will in it, not casually recommending people.' Ouch! And two other quotes: 'Adoration remains a grim duty when it ceases to be a joy; and is twice as much worthwhile under these conditions.' [and] 'What you want is that steadfastness of spirit which is only obtained by <u>realizing</u> the greatness of God and the littleness of everything else except as a means to Him. 12-13-00*

When we visited Bangkok, I discovered close to the Bangkok Christian Guest House, Christ Church. It is an Anglican church. And every chance I had I attended their early Sunday morning English language service. Holy Communion continues to have a strong attraction for me.

One advantage of connecting with Oakhurst Baptist Church was the opportunity to write one or two meditations for their yearly devotional booklets for Lent and Advent. Some 18 years later, I am still writing Advent devotions for them.

McGilvary has a wonderful blend of missionary and Thai professors. I can't say I 'liked' all of them, but most of them were good co-workers and friends. And the same was true for the missionaries associated with the Thailand Baptist Ministries—an organization supporting most Baptist missionaries from around the world who were serving in Thailand. (The exception was Southern Baptists who were not interested in that kind of cooperation.)

I continued to write some for Smyth & Helwys. For instance, I wrote four lessons on the Psalms in 2001.

In the new term, I would be teaching in the M.Div program, specifically classes of New Testament Introduction and Church History I. It is interesting that while my doctoral degree was in systematic theology, I never taught that at McGilvary. My classes were New Testament, Old Testament (Psalms and Wisdom Literature), Church History, and Spirituality. I always enjoyed teaching the Bible classes, but Church History and Spirituality were my favorites.

The house we moved into had character. It was on the McGilvary compound and had been built by missionaries many years before. It was wonderfully convenient to my teaching at the seminary and Pat's ministry at the International School nearby to a special need's child of a Baptist missionary family. It was two stories—with lots of room. However—*We still have a couple of problems with the house. We occasionally have water leaking into the study from the bathroom. And we have rats. We caught one but suspect there are others. We have set some traps and have put poison in the walls. The rats have chewed holes in two curtains and a hole through one of the screens downstairs.* 2-13-01

Pat, as in Bangkok, loved working in the yard—which she did most mornings for a good while. We had flowers and plants that were beautiful.

Yesterday was Songkran—Thai New Year. For three or four days they celebrate by throwing water on one another. So, we joined in the festivities. . .. We rode in the back of a pick-up truck for 3+ hours in the afternoon all throwing and squirting water on folks. We were drenched after the first 10 minutes. Some of the water used was iced—very cold. After freezing [us] for a moment, the cooling water felt good as it cascaded over our bodies. All in all, a good time. 4-14-01

Eventually I started attending an English language Catholic service at a Jesuit retreat center. At first, I did not take Holy Communion, but eventually, encouraged by other Protestants there and being assured that the Jesuits did not care, I began to take Communion. I found the services and the sermons much better than in any other English language services I attended in Chiang Mai.

Gracious God . . . all that is good, true, and beautiful flow from the fount of your radiant nature. I look at the multi-colored plants and blooming flowers in my yard and know their beauty comes from your creative greatness. I see the clouds and the sun moving according to the laws of nature and know their faithfulness reflects your truth. I see my wife gong off to a meeting at school and know that she, my love, shines with your goodness. You are worthy of all praise and honor and glory. . . .. May my thoughts never be far from you or from appreciation of the glimpses of your goodness, truth, and beauty. 6-1-01

At our first annual meeting of TBM, we went to Cha-Am. Among the missionaries we got to know were the Foxes with whom we shared a cabin. They became good friends with whom we spent a couple of Christmases at their house in Chiang Rai. Chuck became a good golf buddy as well.

We loved the international restaurants in Chiang Mai, as well as the less expensive Thai restaurants. We ate out often. We also enjoyed the English language movies at the main mall there. So, it is no surprise that for Pat's birthday one year, we ate Italian at Stephano's and had dessert and coffee at Starbucks. On another birthday we ate a late breakfast at the Garden Restaurant and went to a movie. The only movie showing that we were interested in was Planet of the Apes!

Pat had a variety of jobs in her years in Chiang Mai. Many of them overlapped. She was the person responsible for helping TBM missionaries with special needs children. She led a Thai organization called Christian Tribal Youth Fellowship. She also served for a time as the volunteer coordinator for TBM. She was TBM's representative on the Board of the language school and the Christian Guest House, both in Bangkok. Eventually she became chairperson of TBM with enormous responsibilities.

9-11-2001 was a day that shook America and the world. Here are three journal entries that reflect my own troubled conscience.

Two days ago, we were reminded of how terribly evil human beings can be in a way that none of us will ever forget. People were killed when 4 airplanes were hi-jacked and 3 of them were used to ram into the twin towers of the World Trade Center and the Pentagon. It was certainly the work of Islamic terrorists, probably under the tutelage of a man named bin Laden. I am still somewhat speechless. What can one say but that evil is real? . . . But how are we to respond. As Christian individuals we are called to prayer. Pray for those who lost loved ones and for those injured as they recover and for the emotional suffering that blankets our country. But we must also pray for 'our enemies'. We can pray that those who perpetuated this horrendous act would be seared in their consciences and filled with remorse. We can pray that in humility and brokenness, they would turn to God for forgiveness and a new heart. May it be so. Amen. 9-13-01

Today many Americans face the third temptation of Jesus (Matthew 4:8-10) to follow the ways of Satan—to return evil for evil. May they resist. May God-loving, Jesus-following, Spirit-filled Christians sound the call for mercy even as 'justice' must be sought. . . .. We talked with Jason last night. They leave for Indonesia tomorrow. I pray that they will be protected; that God will watch over them. 9-17-01 (Since retiring, I have joined a small band of people who have a weekly vigil for peace in Birmingham. It was started immediately after 9/11.)

I have always been a conditional pacifist, not an absolute one. My affirmation was and still is that pacifism is the rule that only God can lift. For me that means either some kind of personal revelation or the affirmation by spiritual leaders I respect who with tears call for a just war. In practice that means I would probably rest in my pacifism for my whole life. However, the 'war' against bin Laden and terrorism is hard to argue against except to affirm strongly that innocent life must be spared as far as possible. . ... The magnitude of the cold-blooded decision to kill 1000s of people makes it easier to justify the destruction of the terrorists, but if I, in the end, accept that fact, I will do so with fear and trembling. I will not rejoice at the death of my enemies but will weep for them as well. Help me Lord to know your will; to know the truth. Help me to love my enemies. I pray for bin Laden and terrorists of all stripes. May they be shaken out of their desire for revenge and retaliation. May the Spirit of your love and peace descend on them. May repentance and forgiveness become a reality on all sides. Amen. 9-21-01

I have already mentioned Pat leading the Christian Tribal Youth Fellowship. Sometimes she went to their meetings alone, but I also enjoyed going with her and them on trips once or twice. Most of my life, I have enjoyed being around young people. Of course, it can also become too much of a good thing!

Over the Christmas holidays in 2001, Kari, Patrick, Caitlyn, Jordan, Jason and Lori all visited with us. We did a lot of traveling—Chiang Rai, Pattaya, and Bangkok. If I remember correctly Jordan arrived with a broken leg and the most remembered moment with Caitlyn occurred in Pattaya. Caitlyn (who was 5 or 6) had made a list of things she wanted to do on the beach. When they got down to the beach, she realized that she had forgotten to bring the list. She was upset, but Kari told her that they could probably remember them all. Caitlyn, "But I might get them in the wrong order!"

I finished the second Harry Potter book and quoted from memory that Dumbledore told Harry, "the decisions we make are far more important than the abilities we have." A great truth.

Dad was hospitalized for a short while because he had some mini strokes. A month later, Pat and I went to the States for a short vacation. (It was McGilvary's summer break.) We visited with family and friends. We also stayed with dad at Tom and Jackie's house to give them a couple of days off.

When we returned to McGilvary for the beginning of the new school year, I was excited that 1) I was now in charge of the morning devotions for faculty and staff and 2) I would be doing Communion on Monday mornings at the student hostel. Both responsibilities were blessings to me, and I trust to others.

A quote from Margaret Guenther's book *Toward Holy Ground: Spiritual Directions for the Second Half of Life*, "When we pray for individuals, we should simply bring their names/faces before God and wait with them there. Then close with something like, 'Lord, have mercy' or "Lord, bless him/her.' The point being that we don't really know what their deepest needs are, so it is better to trust God than to try to advise God in these matters."

As the year moved on, I noted how busy I had become with committee meetings. I had been elected as the Fellowship Chairman at the Thailand Baptist Missionary Fellowship annual conference. I was on 7 different committees at McGilvary in addition to being part of two faculties which also had meetings. On top of that I continued to be the advisor for the same class of students—now in their second year. However, for the latter, I committed myself to functioning in a pastoral role for them and not just an administrative one.

I always enjoyed the work trips we made with the students. The students gave up at least part of their vacation time to do ministry and work projects in hill villages. Here is an account of one.

Pat and I are in a mountain Karen village with around 35 students. . . .. We are making a cement floor for [what will be] a children's school. We are about half done. We will finish up today. My lower back was a little sore yesterday from shoveling rock into buckets.

We have morning devotions, evening worship, and work in between. The first morning, the fourth-year students had a program for the children which included handing out some clothes. They also brought clothes and blankets for the adults. We could have used an extra blanket the last couple of nights. It's been pretty chilly. We brought a couple of light blankets, but both of us have been chilly in the early morning hours. This morning I put my jeans over my pajama pants. It helped.

I drove the Binkley's van up. I had trouble in one spot where I had to back up a time or two in order to get up one of the dirt roads on the hill. [There were scary steep drop-offs over the side of the road!] At some point, we had a flat tire but did not realize it until we arrived at the village. We will have new tire going back. 10-10-02

I went to a meeting of Baptist educators in Hong Kong. It was my first trip there and I found it fascinating. *I did find a little souvenir for Pat—her name in Chinese characters on a bookmark. I thought the meaning of the three characters for 'Patricia' were neat: evergreen, green jade, and silky. She is indeed lively, precious, and sensuous.* 1-12-03

America and some allies went to war in Iraq. Here are three quotes which reflect my feelings at the time.

The prospect of war hangs ominously over the world. I am fairly certain it cannot be justified. However, it is true that 9/11 changed America. It has made us more prepared to attack our perceived enemies with a holy and righteous vengeance. To my eyes it is not a pretty sight. May the Son of God's grace burn brighter in our and their lives. 1-29-03

I pray today for the Church—my brothers and sisters in Christ. May God protect Her and give Her strength to bear witness to His love during these terrible days of terror and war. I pray for the innocents—Christian and non-Christian—who face misery and death because of the mindless violence of terrorism and war. May God have mercy on them. . .. I fear that once released, the dogs of war will not only wreak havoc around the world, but they will birth litters of mangy curs who will perpetuate the hatred and animosity that so marks our present world. God have mercy. 3-8-02

I pray first for the Iraqi Christians. May they be spared from the destruction raining down on Baghdad and Iraq. May they be protected from any reprisals and hatred that come from their Muslim countrymen. And I pray for all Iraqi non-combatants. May they be spared as much as possible from death and destruction. I pray the same for journalists and other non-combatants associated with the Western forces. I pray also for the soldiers. I pray that the coalition forces would be filled with wisdom and compassion. Protect not only their bodies but also their souls. Even in victory may they be able to weep for the slaughter of human beings. I pray for the Iraqi soldiers. They too need wisdom. May they see the futility of their fight. May they surrender without further bloodshed. And finally, I pray 'deliver us from evil'. May the evil in Iraq and the evil in American be transformed [into goodness, love and peace]. 3-24-03

But all was not doom and gloom in March of 2003. While in the States, I got to baptize Caitlyn. It was a wonderful day.

Back in Thailand, I had some problem with a recurring foot infection. I was planning to go to Ram Hospital. *I tossed and turned last night with some worry about my foot. I don't want to tell Pat about the worry because it is too much like my dad! However, my worry meter is a bit odd. Once I get under a doctor's care, I rarely worry much at all. Now I suppose if they can't find out what the problem might be, I might continue to worry, but that has not happened to me very much. I don't know if I worry more about stuff like that now. I hope not, since if it is increasing with age, I won't be able to sleep at all when I am 70!* 11-22-03 I have to chuckle about this quote. As I write this I am 71. Unfortunately, my ability to worry, especially about illnesses at night, continues unabated. But at least it hasn't gotten worse.

2004 started with a bang! Nico was born in Chiang Mai at 7 am on January 15, 2004. Pat and I were so glad they all could stay with us in those first months.

In March we planned to visit Ireland on our way back to the States for furlough. We fell in love with the country and its people. We visited Dublin, Waterford, Limerick and Galway— followed by tours of Connemara and the Cliffs of Moher.

Only one quote and comment from our visit. This concerning our time in Dublin *We went into the city this afternoon. We had some pub food with Guinness for lunch. Then we went to Trinity College. The Book of Kells exhibit was impressive. The funny thing was how quiet everyone was as we made our way through the exhibit to the actual book. It was as though a kind of holy wonder permeated the place. The hours and hours of work that went into creating this masterpiece is impressive. I cannot assume that all who worked on it were equally spiritual, but it must have felt like holy work to most if not all.* 3-27-04 This was followed by a visit to another room which held 200,000 of the oldest books at the college. I was in awe!

Furloughing in the States

We stayed in a mission house owned by Wieuca Road Baptist Church. It was a Cooperative Baptist Church, but quite willing to let us American Baptist missionaries stay there. It was in a beautiful part of Atlanta and it was within walking distance of a Borders Book Store—one of my favorites, that alas has gone out of business.

We enjoyed spending time with our family, including dad, who was in an assisted living facility—which he loved! Of course, the most fun was being with Caitlyn and Jordan!

However, there were some difficult times related to the mission board. They had feared that lay-off might be necessary. Fortunately, that did not happen. However, the board did decide that missionaries had to begin raising most of their finances—at least in terms of salary. To do this they suggested forming Missionary Partnership Teams who would be responsible for helping to raise the money, especially when we missionaries returned to our fields. Our MPT was centered in West Virginia where we had some former missionary teams and where we would be spending a lot of our deputation time. We loved spending time in beautiful West Virginia and visiting many churches. But unfortunately, our MPT never really got off the ground.

To make matters worse, the board fired the fairly new Executive Director who was Hispanic—the first non-Caucasian to fill the position. It caused quite a stir among the Hispanic Caucus of American Baptist Churches.

The spiritual highlight of my time in the States that furlough was a retreat at a monastery in Conyers, Georgia. Catherine Powell, whom I had met at the Mars Hill gatherings years before directed four or five of us retreatants all individually. It was a Cistercian monastery which means that the monks practiced silence most of the day and night except for worship times.

I am sitting at my little desk in my room at the monastery in Conyers. I arrived this afternoon and met with Cathy about 4. She gave some suggested scripture for use between now and tomorrow about 4. She also suggested three periods of prayer not longer than 45 minutes each unless God was leading to stay with it. This is a Cistercian monastery, so I am surrounded by silence. I can hear the scraping of pen point on paper. 12-6-04

Two other remembrances from that wonderful retreat:

Two or three days after the retreat began, one of the scripture passages that had been given to me for that day was Ezekiel 36:25-28a where God promised to give Israel a new heart—a heart of flesh in place of a heart of stone. *In my meditation, I saw God remove from my chest a heart of stone. I thought he would throw it away and give me the heart of flesh. Instead, he took my stone heart and placed it next to his chest. He held it there and it was transformed. Perhaps it was my original heart decalcified. Or maybe not. But it was at least my old heart given new life and pliability. May the vision be true. Thank you, gracious, gracious God for a heart warmed by your Presence.* 12-8-04

A note from my last morning there; *After a quiet breakfast, I walked out into the little garden or grotto. . .. It is foggy today. It is easy to see up close. Distances are a bit fuzzy. Maybe that in itself is a spiritual truth. Be present. Be now with Christ and allow the fuzzy distances to wait for the next day or the next. I walked around the enclosed area looking at the statues, rock gardens, bonsai trees, and other things. When I stood still I could hear the geese squawking to God for their food. Then in the silence I could hear the heavy dew dripping, dripping off the trees—an abundance of moisture like an abundance of grace. Thank you, Father.* 12-9-04

Of course, it was in December of 2004 that disaster struck Indonesia where Jason and Lori were serving as missionaries.

Fortunately, they were away at the time on vacation in Thailand.

It is ironic that in the aftermath of the great earthquake and tsunami, that Psalm 46 is this morning's reading; 'God is our refuge and strength, a very present help in trouble. Therefore, we will not fear, though the earth be moved, and though the mountains be toppled into the depths of the sea. Though its waters rage and foam, and though the mountains tremble at its tumult.' The language is intended as metaphorical. The writer is affirming his belief that God will protect Jerusalem. However, what can these words mean to millions in Asia who are suffering so? How did Israel chant these words after the fall of Jerusalem? This morning I don't seem to have any good answers—only stuff that sounds trite in my head. So, I came to the last part of the psalm; 'Be still, then, and know that I am God; I will be exalted among the nations.' Out of the rubble of destruction may the peoples of South and Southeast Asia find You. May they experience your love and your peace. Amen. Jason has traveled to Banda Aceh. Gracious Lord protect him from all evil. May your Name be exalted in his service to the needy. 12-31-04

We returned to Thailand in April of 2005 by way of Ireland and Scotland. The highlight of our Ireland leg was visiting the town of Sligo. We saw some fine architecture there including a statue of W. B. Yeats wrapped in his words. We attended a Methodist church service on Sunday, followed by bar food for lunch. It was a family affair with children and parents and grandparents gathering there. A jazz and blues group played and sang there every Sunday afternoon.

In Scotland, we stayed with old friends who we had gotten to know as missionaries in Thailand—the Fucellas. They lived in Edenborough—an awesome city to walk around.

Back in Chiang Mai

The next 3 plus years are our last in Thailand as missionaries. Perhaps it is best just to summarize my work at McGilvary during that last term.

I continued to love being there—most days. The divinity school started a new English language program; The International M.Div Program. The classes and seminars were all taught in English. We had students from a variety of countries, but the bulk were from Vietnam and Myanmar. I enjoyed getting to teach in English. My classes included courses in spirituality, church history, Bible, and philosophy.

I also still had responsibilities in the Thai M.Div program. In addition to being a student advisor, I went with students for their Sunday church work and I attended work camps and retreats. These included retreats for first year students, for faculty, and for the International students. I also continued the once-a-month Communion services at the student hostel. I opened up the once-a-week evening English language contemplative Taize-style service to students who might want to attend.

Two other items to mention. Bill Yoder, long time head of the divinity school retired. The new administration was not as cordial. They were often frustrating to me and to others of the faculty. Additionally, strains in the faculty became more apparent. While I continued to enjoy teaching and working with students, this new atmosphere was depressing.

On a more positive note, I finished work on a book about Asian Church History. The book was an enlargement of my notes from the class I taught. Of course, it was written in English. When I left, the Korean professor who replaced me in teaching Asian Church History used those notes. Attempts were made to translate the book into Thai, but I don't think the project was ever completed. More about this book in about 14 years!

On the home front in the States, my dad had a stroke and eventually wound up in a nursing home. Tom's wife, Jackie, was the head nurse there, so she took good care of him. And

Tom was a regular visitor. I visited when home for short summer vacations.

Also, Pat's dad, who had remarried, developed a terminal cancer. Pat was able to be with him for an extended period before he passed away. We lost both of our dads in these years.

Now a few quotes and a few other snippets of memories.

We went out for a dinner last night. We went to La Crystal—a French restaurant. It was the most expensive meal we have ever had around $125. A fifth of that was a half a bottle of wine. However, the food was good, the atmosphere was nice with a jazz/pop trio, and the service was perfect. We talked a bit about our 37 years of marriage and just enjoyed each other's company. 8-2-05

I attended a church sponsored camp in the Chiang Rai, along with three others from McGilvary.

The tribal group is Chin Haw, . . . however many of the students are Akha. Considering that they are teenagers, and most are not Christian, they seemed to listen to a lot of what I said this afternoon. I was on for one and a half hours. . . . I have missed Pat here but have had a good time. . . . However, I felt like I was hitting a tolerance wall an hour or so ago. However, we are over half-finished. We worship tonight and tomorrow. We will probably have some more games and vcd times. We will also have group devotions in the morning. I did not feel I did well with that at all this morning. . . . [But] the camp has seemed to go well. 9-10-05

At the close of Boonyawat's message Saturday night, an invitation was issued. 15 or 20 came forward and knelt in prayer. He asked me to pray over them. Because of my Thai, that was probably not the best choice though I prayed with sincerity and am certain God listened. I continue to pray for those kids that 1) there would be some kind of follow up, 2) that they would grow in Christ, and 3) that God would preserve them through any kind of family or peer pressure that would draw them away from the Way. 9-13-05

I have been asked to preach in English in chapel next Thursday. I am glad to do so, but it is still a bit of work since they want a detailed outline in Thai to put in the bulletin. So, I worked on that yesterday and should finish it today. It will be a full day with morning faculty prayers at 8, classes from 9:30 to 11:00 and 3:00-5:00, and faculty meeting from 1:30 to 3:00! But the weekend is near, hopefully followed by golf Monday morning. I have a wonderful life—teaching, loving, and playing—all hopefully covered by devotion to God and experiences of abundant grace. Thank you, my Lord. 10-28-05

I am preaching the next two Sundays. Tomorrow I will be preaching at a church belonging to the Church of Christ in the Philippines. It is where Sumali [one of my students] works. Next Sunday, I will be in a CCT church where Duangsuda [one of our professors] is a member. They will be concluding a weekend revival. I will lead the Communion service. They have asked me to baptize a three-month-old, but I had to decline. 11-26-05

We continued to enjoy getting away for vacation from the heat of Thailand to the wonderful coolness of the Malaysian Cameron Highlands. In mid-December of 2005 we spent the time in the Malaysia with Jason, Lori, Nico, the Kinnisons, and the Cranes. As I recall, the golf course was soaking wet and my game was terrible, but still it was a good time with family and friends.

Yesterday I was the first one downstairs and had a time of being alone with some hot tea and a view of mountains and fog. This morning I was a little slower and can hear movement downstairs. I think I will shower before going down. Hmmm, I smell muffins. Better hurry while they are hot! 12-11-05

We have enjoyed the fireplace, reading, music, conversation, and good meals. We have also been playing cards at night. It has been a nice vacation with good friends. Thank you, Lord. 12-14-05

Pat's jobs continued to change. She had taught English at McGilvary before our last term. The students called her an angel! She helped two or three pass the required English course which they had previously failed. She became the coordinator for volunteers for Thailand Baptist Mission Fellowship. I took over the English classes.

Pat and I went to a work camp in a Karen village in March of 2006. The afternoon temperatures were probably over 100 degrees, but the mornings were nice. One night the students did skits. Some of them did a skit of Pat and me—an imaginative reenactment of our meeting, courtship, wedding, and life. It was really cute. Wish we had taped it!

In the Thai 'summer' we went back to the States for deputation work. But it certainly wasn't all work! *All things are temporary, but we can properly evaluate what should be of utmost importance. Nevertheless, we can also enjoy the temporal blessings of life; the little things that are destined to fade away. So, I thank You today Lord for the strong taste of my coffee, the sweet crunchiness of my scone, the sound of running water, the quiet ambience of JaMoka's, and this moment in which the Eternal sits at table with me.* 4-11-06

A note from our return trip to Thailand while we had a stopover in Taipei, Taiwan: *Flying has been rather comfortable this time with very little serious turbulence. In fact, I have been in more danger walking! In the LA airport, I managed to stumble over a metal table and hit the floor. I have a bruise and contusion on my left shin and scrapes and bruises on my right elbow. But it could have been worse. I told Pat I was doing my Chevy Chase imitation.* 5-11-06

I [sometimes] write as though I am a person of great faith or as one with sublime spiritual experiences. But many times, I don't feel that way. Sometimes I fear I am only writing pious platitudes that have little bearing on who I really am Too often, it seems to me, I am touched with confusion and doubt. I cannot tell where these come from. Are they God's Spirit convicting me? Are they the works of Satan to cause me to stumble? Are they simply the psychological results of my conservative SBC upbringing coupled with experiences in the wider world? Who shall deliver me from this web of confusion? Only Jesus, only Jesus. 5-25-06

A few days later, I was at a retreat for first year students in the hills. *There is a picture in the house where we slept. It is a plain picture of Jesus on the cross. At the top of the picture is a simple, but profound inscription: 'The God'. I saw and I read. My heart leaped. My spirit responded to the truth. This was not only a great man. This was and is my God.* 5-31-06

One morning doing my devotions, apparently at Starbucks in Chiang Mai, I read psalm 98. The translation I used that day read this way for verse 1, "The mercies of the LORD are new every morning and thus a new song is due for the great things he has done." *There is the very fact of love. Specifically love between Pat and me. Even as she is flying to be with her dad this morning, that love is real and binds us together. [Then there is] the love of our kids. . .. There is the fact of nature; the blue sky, the clouds, the amazing variety of green life growing outside Starbucks' window. And then what can one say about cinnamon rolls, coffee, and sweet music. Thank You Lord. Thank You for the great big blessings and for the small, marvelous ones. Amen.* 6-25-06

In July of 2006, I was working on an essay on how my understanding of the Lord's Supper has changed over the years. It was eventually published in a book of essays by the Trinity Group entitled "For Faith and Friendship". It was dedicated to one of our group who was dying of cancer, Philip Wise. He continues to be missed.

In August of that year, the Cranes stayed with us for a few weeks while the birth of Jaden neared. We really enjoyed having them around. Jaden was born on August 8.

Yesterday in the International class, we did Lectio Divina from 1 John 1:1-4. The phrase I meditated on was "we have . . . touched with our hands." This quickly transformed into "I touched with my hands." Two images came to mind. 1) The Lord's Supper in which I hold the Bread of Life and 2) the needy that I lay hands on in prayer and blessing. Thank you for these two experiences of communion with You. May I never ignore one. 11-23-06

Yesterday Saddam Hussein was executed. The report said that there was fear in his eyes as the end approached. And well there might have been. By all accounts, he was an evil man. But darkness cannot be overcome by darkness. The Roman Catholics are correct to call for an end to the death penalty. Oh God, convict the many Fundamentalists and Evangelicals who cannot yet see that truth. I pray that before I die I will see at least the majority of Christians rejecting the 'final' solution of execution. 12-31-06

My dad passed away in early March of 2007. Tom and I did the funeral which was a simple graveside service. A reflection a few days later; *I was thinking in the last few days about my dad. In some ways his life was like a dream. It will not be remembered—at least beyond a generation or two. He left no great work to be remembered by. That does not mean his life was insignificant. His influence for good will continue to be experienced in the world as long as his children pass on his commitment to faithfulness toward family and church. I am at the student work camp and realize anew from today's reading in Psalm 90 that my own life is short, and I must make use of the time. In my case it means helping to prepare these students so that their lives will count for Christ and His Church. Help me Lord to be faithful to the work you have graciously given me to do.* 3-17-07

I love the writings of Evelyn Underhill. I wish I could have sat in on one of the many retreats that she offered. In lieu of that I am thankful I have books that contain some of the material she used. *I read a retreat presentation by Underhill on prayer. She emphasized the absolute importance of adoration. I have said many times that adoration does not come naturally to Americans. [It is easier for people in hierarchical cultures.] We have to work at it. I don't think that is a contradiction in terms; 'work at praise'. It was an old English mystic, Richard Rolle, who encouraged people to voice short affirmations of love toward God often. By such practice, the reality of love would gradually be formed in our lives. How wonderful it would be if it could all be spontaneous all the time. But has it ever been so—even for the saints and mystics?* 3-31-07

Pat's dad passed away about a little over a month after mine. *Pat's dad passed away Saturday night (Thai time). After a long search, we were finally able to get tickets for her back to Bangkok and Chiang Mai. She should be in the air now. May God watch over her and protect her. I feel like I may be depressed—probably very mild. I seem to be struggling more with doubts lately wondering about God and 'heaven'; fearing that death could be the end. But this morning I used some of the Easter Season liturgy from the Book of Common Prayer. It was good to affirm with Christians around the world: "Alleluia! Christ is risen. The Lord is risen indeed. Alleluia! Thanks be to God who gives us the victory through our Lord Jesus Christ." I believe; help my unbelief. Amen.* 4-16-07

Pat had neck surgery in September of 2007. She had it in Bangkok. Everything went well. The doctors, staff, and hospital were great.

I noted that same month, I saw a book on writing haiku. I didn't buy it, but I did compose one in my head as I lay in bed one night. My first haiku—not written down and lost forever! Later in the States, haiku will become an important part of my spiritual life.

A prayer of praise and thanksgiving: *Father, I praise You as the Creator of all things. I praise You as the One who provides for your children, your creation. I praise you that I might call you Father in the most intimate way because of your Son and your Spirit. Blessed Son, I worship You. You are my Savior and my Lord. By your death and resurrection, I have been and will be saved from sin and death. You love and mercy are immeasurable. Incarnate Jesus, you are also our perfect Example. I praise You for bringing me to the Father and giving me your Spirit. Holy and awesome Spirit, I adore you. You give me Life deeper than mere existence. By You, through You, my life has meaning beyond the physical and temporary. You have filled me with Eternal Life brightly colored with love, joy, and peace. And in this life through You, I know (I experience) the Father and the Son. Glorious God; Father, Son, and Holy Spirit; may the words I have written be pleasing to You. I know they will be appropriate only if they come from my heart. And my heart will only be right as You abide therein. Bless me Lord that I might truly bless You and be a blessing to others. Amen.* 11-10-07

On the 28th I noted several things in my journal, two of which were especially important to me: 1) Alex and Bella had been born the day before on Thai time! 2) One of my Vietnamese students who had graduated was going to teach a course on spirituality at a Bible college in Cambodia.

We were able to take a short vacation during the Christmas holiday of 2007. We had a great time. *Bella and Alex are wonderful. They are both adorable. I will miss them when we return to Thailand.* 12-20-07. Also, during that holiday, the whole family, except the twins and Lori, went to Pigeon Forge and had nice time.

Back in Thailand at a work camp in March, I got nipped by a little dog. I think I stepped on him. Anyway, I didn't think much about until I got home where Pat was concerned about rabies. She was right to be. I read later that rabies was not uncommon in the mountains of northern Thailand. So, I got rabies shots, which were not painful, and all was good.

I was thinking about living back in the US and my own distaste for patriotism and nationalism. Israel was, in some special sense, chosen by God. While their nationalistic pride could sometimes become unendearing, I can understand their sense of specialness before God. . ... But America's 'God and Country' celebrations, I hate. America as a nation is no more special to God that Gambia as a nation. Certainly, Americans are no more loved by God than Karen and Lahu. I am grateful for the advantages of being born in America. But I am more thankful that I have gotten to know and appreciate other nations and peoples. I am first a citizen of heaven, then of the world. American citizenship is a reality for me, but it is not high on my list of important things. 4-24-08

It was during this time period that Pat and I began to think about returning to the States to stay. It was a long hard decision and not decided until we were back in the States for several months. Pat felt strongly that we needed to be in the States. I went back and forth, especially as we returned for our furlough—which turned out to be our last. There were some pretty tense moments between the two of us. But I am getting ahead of myself!

Jesus talked about 'sowing and reaping' in John 4: 27-42. I asked myself where I fit in that analogy. *I have done little of either. Though that is true only if one think in terms of 'soul-winning'. I have planted [I hoped] a crop of 'Jesus loving' flowers that would blossom. That is my desire; that the world would love and praise and exalt the name of Jesus. May I be an example—a winsome one—of such a flower.* 6-24-08

Stateside

One of the issues that had concerned Pat was some memory problems I seemed to be having. So, in late December, we went to a gerontologist. He affirmed that I did not have Alzheimer's and cognitively was pretty normal for 61. Eventually, my memory lapses improved, so perhaps they were caused by stress.

Another health problem was beginning to surface. I was having some pains in my back and hips. I assumed it was related to a pinched nerve. I was wrong. But first, our search for a new pastorate.

The first church that we looked at was an American Baptist Church in West Virginia. We met with the committee, surveyed the community of Oak Hill, and eventually I preached for the committee. They wanted to have me come to preach at the church in view of a call. In the end, I turned them down. Part of the decision was because some of the committee expressed hope that I could get the music director and pianist to use more contemporary music. I didn't want to get into that battle! However, the main reason was probably that I was still hoping we might return to Chiang Mai.

The next church was First Baptist in Bunkie. It was a Southern Baptist Church but had some folks in the church who had supported the more moderate professors at New Orleans Baptist Seminary and Louisiana Baptist College in Alexandria in their struggle with Fundamentalists who had wanted them fired.

A late entry was my old church First Baptist of Montezuma. Eventually, I called the chairperson of the Pastor Search Committee—a friend of ours, Jule Windham. He indicated that there were only two names they were considering. One was

Randy Gregg who was pastor before I went there the first time. He had become the interim pastor when the last pastor left and decided to throw his hat in the ring. He was also still a member of the church. Jule said that he was the only member of the committee who had ever served on a Pastor Search Committee. He told me that the committee looked like deer caught in headlights! They didn't know what to do. Eventually, I told them to call Randy and that I would go to Bunkie which had already issued a call for me to come as their pastor.

In the meantime, I had recently sent my resignation into the Board. International Ministries gave us six months to find a job during which time we would still receive salary and benefits, e.g., insurance coverage.

Shortly after I resigned, the Executive Director sent out a notice that six of the staff at the Board would be laid off at the end of the week and that all missionaries would have to raise 100% of their support by the Fall of 2009. We would never have been able to do that, so I don't really know what might have happened, but we never had to find out.

I remain thankful for International Ministries of American Baptist Churches which has a commitment to collaborative work alongside national partners—a commitment that was missing from some other mission organizations who were too focused on a Fundamentalist understanding of scripture and theology to work with national partners who took different approaches. They also understood that their mandate in missions included not only evangelism and church planting, but also helping ministries that did not have to be successful in starting churches in order to justify their existence.

Our lives began to change drastically on March 5, 2009. I went to see a neurologist in Atlanta. I had assumed my issues were the result of a pinched nerve. However, when she heard my symptoms, she tested my right leg and my lower back. She noticed some weakness in the lower part of my leg. Then she found a tremor in my left foot. She said that I might have ALS—commonly referred to as Lou Gehrig's disease. I asked her if Pat would join us so the doctor could explain it to both of us. When Pat heard the news, she asked the doctor if ALS was like Parkinson's disease. She said that in some ways it was, but that ALS usually progressed much faster—3 to 5 years was the norm.

There was still the possibility that my symptoms were caused by a pinched nerve—though she did not think so. An MRI was scheduled but could not happen until after a final trip to Chiang Mai to take care of some final matters before leaving for good.

Yesterday I moved out of my office [in Chiang Mai] and turned in my keys. It was like a death. But later I reflected that for the Christian, resurrection follows death like morning follows night. In the months ahead I will have life in a new ministry 3-25-09

On our last day in Chiang Mai, I had two journal entries. In the morning, I wrote, *it is our last Saturday here. I know my emotional state is very fragile; Philip's death [who had died a few days earlier], my own disease, and leaving Thailand. Gracious God, I pray for your blessings in the months and years to come. I pray to You who have blessed me with a wonderful wife and family, a healthy 60 years, a meaningful and joyful ministry in Thailand and the prospects of ministry in Bunkie. My life has been good. No matter what the future holds, my life will have been good. Thank You. Amen.* 4-5-09

Then later in the afternoon, I wrote, *I am feeling melancholy, depressed, and scared again. I haven't felt this way in several days. I can feel a lot of twitching in my legs. I am having some muscle spasms in my leg and arm. . . . I feel tense, sweaty. It is the sweat of fear, I think. Last night I fell asleep but woke up after midnight and seemed to struggle to sleep again. I have not had the shivers and shakes [as I did in the days immediately after the first neurologist visit], but I feel like I could at any time. My thoughts have not been as dark as in the early days after the possibility of disease and death were affirmed. But my ability to find peace;*

to quiet my mind is not working very well. . .. I feel weepy, weak. It is embarrassing in some ways. I find myself looking for the twitches. Help me Lord. I know You love me. Whatever may come, may I never doubt Your love. Lord Jesus be my song and my strength and my salvation. Amen. 4-5-09 The last sentence is a version of my theme verse which I used on all of my name cards from my first pastorate in Tangipahoa. It is from Psalm 118:14 (RSV).

We got the results from the MRI on the 17th of April. There was no pinched nerve. The fear of ALS returned in full force. *I did not rest as well last night as I had been. I thought of insurance concerns. I thought of conversations I could/would be having with folks— and dreading them. I thought of Bunkie and how all of this would affect my ministry there. And I though again of a quick death being preferable— maybe.* 4-18-09 The thought of a quick death related to how terrible the disease becomes as it progresses.

My first thought when I got up this morning was "I am dying." Now that is a depressing way to begin the day. It may be true and if it is, I need to come to grips with that reality. But I would prefer praise to be my first thought. I did quickly move to thanksgiving and praise, but the first thought was a bit disconcerting. 4-19-09

This morning I plan to start a thanksgiving list on my computer. I have so much to be thankful for. It will be chronological. . .. I am doing this in part as following Paul's old admonition:" Do not worry about anything, but in everything by prayer and supplication with thanksgiving let your requests be made known to God. And the peace of God which surpasses all understanding, will guard your hearts and your minds in Christ Jesus." [Phil. 4:6-7] . . . Those verses have stood me in good stead over the years and I want to continue to follow the pattern. Thank You for this day Lord. Thank You for my sweet wife and wonderful family. Amen. 4-20-09

I started the list and have continued to update it over the years. It continues to be a blessing.

First Baptist Church, Bunkie, Louisiana

In May, we moved to Montezuma to begin my work there as pastor. We were there for 3 years and 4 months. As with any pastorate, there were good times and bad times, positive and negative experiences. Without slogging through a lot of quotes from my journals, I will attempt to simply describe some of those experiences.

I want to begin with some of the negative ones, because I would like to think it is the positive ones which will stay with me and warm my heart.

The bane of my existence at the church turned out to be the minister of music. He refused any suggestions I made about hymns or special music. He believed that he was the expert in music, and I should mind my own business! He also planned some features in the worship service without running them by me.

Eventually, he complained to the music committee about me 'interfering' with his music program. We had some meetings and the committee encouraged him to work more closely with me, but it did not happen.

The problem was exacerbated by the fact that a small, but influential group in the church, sided with him. Eventually, every time any issue would arise in deacons' meetings or business meetings, these 8 or so people would oppose my position. Three of the men were deacons. One couple eventually left the church. Another husband died. The others stayed in the church. Several of them were choir members. I kept thinking the minister of music would leave, but he outlasted me! But after I left, he finally went a step too far and resigned when he didn't get his way.

The great majority of the congregation were politically conservative—pro-Republican and anti-Obama. Even with some of my friends I found myself arguing for the need to maintain government safety nets for the poor and the disabled. Of course, I agreed with them that some people abused the system but insisted that the good it did should not be eliminated.

The other issue was my fault for not understanding the Baptist culture in the church. Historically, the Baptists and other Protestants had been abused by the predominate Roman Catholic presence in that part of Louisiana and further south. Memories were long. One of the things that I looked at was how to grow the church. It seemed to me that one area of possible growth was with disaffected Catholics in the area. Since I already had a strong attachment to Holy Communion, we started having it once a month. We also incorporated more liturgy in the church. I had thought about starting the weekly Communion service like I had at Montezuma, but something happened that made me rethink my approach.

The first Good Friday that I was pastor there, I decided to have a Good Friday service—which the church had never experienced. I also decided to use the intinction method where people would come forward to receive a wafer from a plate held by our Chairman of Deacons and dip it in a cup held by me. The church was almost packed. After the service I received several positive complements and thought I was on the right track.

But a storm was brewing. At our next deacons' meeting, one of the deacons read an anonymous letter attacking the service as tainted with Roman Catholicism and being non-Baptist. One of the deacons rose to the occasion and demanded to know who had written the letter because they would not put any stock in anonymous letters. It turns out the letter was written by the wife of the deacon who read it. While nothing came of it, it was clear to me that I needed to dial back the supposedly Catholic elements in our services. Too many, even of my supporters, feared we might lose members. So, needless to say, we never had Communion by intinction again and I never started the weekly Communion service.

Now on to the positives, and they were significant. The vast majority of the deacons supported me when issues were raised. We had a wonderful group of people with whom we became good friends. We baptized a good number of people in the time I was there and had others to join the church by transfer of letter. And we had some folks to begin attending again who had left for various reasons. The church bought a projector and screen which I enjoyed using to display my sermon outlines and images related to the sermon. I had a good weekly ministry at the Bailey House—a residential place for people who could not stay at home but weren't ready for a nursing home. I enjoyed visiting in homes and hospitals—and always felt welcomed. I could go on and on, but finally, the church was wonderfully supportive when the diagnosis of ALS was confirmed. They supported Pat and me in wonderful ways that I will never forget.

Now some more personal and family notes.

When I was diagnosed with ALS, Pat decided that getting Korat cats like we had in Thailand would be comforting for me. She also thought we might make some extra funds. The extra funds plan worked until the country had an economic downturn. Then it was all we could do to give kitten away!

Our first kitten was Suni which Pat picked up in El Paso. Sometime later that year, she flew to Chicago and got Jinx, a male kitten. Then in December we drove to Fayetteville to pick up our second female which we named Didi. All were registered Korats.

Our old friend, John Simmons from American Baptist days in Thailand suggested that I contact our Ministers and Missionaries Benefits Board representative to talk about insurance. I did and we were able to get some insurance for me that did not cost an arm and a leg! Related to my physical situation, we did see a neurologist in Lafayette and the tests he ran also suggested that I probably had ALS.

In August of 2009, I found the golf course near Bunkie. It was a nine-hole course with eighteen places to tee off from. Traditionally, Catholic priests were treated well in Catholic areas. This often included no golf green fees. So, one of the advantages of living in that area of Louisiana was that as a minister, I was also given free access to the course—only having to pay for a golf cart if I used one. One of the younger deacons at the church also played golf, so when he wasn't working in the sugar cane fields, we would often play together.

Sunday I will begin my sermons on Matthew 5-7. I anticipate some dissatisfaction as it will talk about mourning and mercy. I will mention mourning over the destruction caused by 'shock and awe' [the whole-sale bombing of Iraq's capital city]. And I will affirm the rightness of Scotland showing mercy to a convicted Libyan bomber who is dying of cancer. But some will get the picture—at least that is my prayer. 8-28-09

I can note here that I always experienced push-back wherever I preached or taught from the Sermon on the Mount. Far too many people simply reject the call of Jesus to non-violence and forgiveness.

I felt like the symptoms of ALS were increasing with twitches in my torso and neck. The neurologist believed it was time to get an appointment at the ALS clinic at Methodist Hospital in Houston. So, we did.

We went to Houston on January 11th and had a battery of tests over two or three days. They included needles (one a bit painful under my tongue), electric shock test, spinal tap, blood work and breathing test. We met with the members of Dr Appel's ALS team. The diagnosis was early-stage ALS in all four quadrants.

I have been thinking lately about how to help Pat and the kids to work through this without losing faith in or love for God. For me, the answer is Jesus. Looking at him, I see the great measure of God's love for me even if the present circumstances can cloud my mind. But it's not just a matter of thought; it also touches the heart. Last night Pat fell apart for awhile with bitter tears. I pray that God will touch her and bring her comfort. May her relationship with God not be disturbed permanently by this disease. And, of course, I pray the same for Kari and Jason. 1-14-10

After a long bout with cancer, Tom's wife, Jackie passed away on February 17, 2010.

With the affirmation of my ALS, I told my local doctor the news. When I did, he eventually told me about his wife. She had an occasional healing ministry. She only did this for people she felt that God wanted her to pray for. He asked if I would like for him to mention my case to her. I agreed. Several days later she called me and said that she would see me at their house.

I went to see Melissa Lavergne. . . .. She said she only saw a few people each year and always prayed before she accepted any who were recommended to her. . . .. She did not always feel led to pray for each one, but she did in my case. She asked my age, how the disease began, what my symptoms were, and what ALS was like (since she knew very little about it). I answered all her questions and told her that the end usually came as the patient's lungs could no longer work and his swallowing muscles also failed. She held my fingers and prayed. Then she moved to my right hand. She held my calves and prayed. Then she moved up my arms and onto my shoulders. Finally, she stood behind me. (I was seated.) She laid her hands on my chest and then moved up to my neck. At the beginning I could hear her vocalizing, but it was soft. At other times she was quiet. At one point she told me that Catholics often got nervous around speaking in tongues, so she had learned to do it silently. After she had prayed over my shoulders, she asked me if I had had problems there or weakness in my arms. I said I had. She replied that her hands got unusually warm on my shoulders. When she finished laying on of hands, she asked me if a lot of people knew about my condition. I said yes. She affirmed that she had seen a large number of people praying. Light was flowing from them up and around me. She also told me of another vision she had in the process [of praying for me]. She had seen a shepherd's gate like she had never seen before. It was solid gold with vines and grapes winding over it. She said it was beautiful. Having a conversation with God, she told Him that she had never seen His gate like that. He said it was not His shepherd gate, but mine! I understood it as an affirmation of my ministry. She also said she was praying for my wife and children. She said something about having prayed a hedge prayer around me to protect me from evil spirits. And she said she would continue to pray for me and if my condition deteriorated, she wanted me to call her and we would pray some more 3-5-10

It is possible, perhaps likely, that this experience was the beginning of my healing. However, it was over a year later that I was declared ALS free. By that time, I had largely forgotten about Melissa Lavergne and her prayers.

In May of 2010 I was invited to join a monthly meeting in Baton Rouge. We met in Malcolm Tolbert's apartment in a wonderful, assisted living place. Fisher Humphreys, Carlton Winberry (another professor from New Orleans), Roger Sullivan (who became our financial advisor and good friend), and a couple of other guys made up the normal gathering. We met and talked about whatever, then when out to lunch. It was a really good group.

In June of 2010, we visited with Jason and his family in Singapore. From there we went to spend a few days in Chiang Mai. I had understood that the personnel committee at Bunkie had given me permission to go. But when I got back there had been an uproar. (Two of the members, including the chairman, were supporters of the music director against me.) The treasurer came to me after we got back and told me that the chairman of the committee had told him not to pay me for those two weeks because I did not have permission to go. He paid me anyway. The matter was brought to the deacons and they overwhelmingly supported my right to go. We lost one couple from the church over that issue. I wasn't sad to see them go! And the deacons voted to give me one more week of vacation for the 2010 year. Some of the deacons came to my office in the days that followed to encourage me.

A quote from one of my favorite Medieval mystics, John Tauler, *for as the height of a tree depends on the depths of its roots, in the same way, the heights we attain in this life are only as great as our humility is deep.* 9-24-10

After the funeral of Frank Thompson, a man well loved by his friends and family, I wrote, *Of course only a handful of people are remembered over the generations. In 100 years, Frank will probably be forgotten—and me too—unless we turn up as a name in someone's genealogical tree. But that is okay too, for we will be 'remembered' by God. We will be united with Him in some wonderful way forever living days full of meaning and glory.* 2-16-11

My thoughts swirled around political issues and economic realities today, but I don't feel the need to write about it. I know Jesus wouldn't vote Republican. He might vote Green over Democrat. I am in danger of making Jesus over in my image!!! Heck, he might not vote at all. 4-19-11

One morning after church I was walking back to the house with one of my deacon friends, Marion Townsend. We commented about how good the day was. I remarked that one thing would make it even better. He asked, "What?" I replied, "If we didn't have to come back tonight!" He laughingly agreed, and things were set in motion.

At the next meeting, he said that he wanted to present a question with an aside, "I'm probably going to hell for this". The question was about discontinuing Sunday night services.

After a month or two of discussion, the deacons and the church agree to my following suggestions: 1) Cancel Sunday night services which would allow us to do some other things. 2) We would meet in homes one Sunday night a month. 3) We would start a pastor's class on Sunday mornings at 8:30. 4) We would lengthen our children's program to year-round without the summer break.

The pastor's class began in September with good attendance. I loved teaching this class for the rest of our time at Bunkie.

Around mid-2011, one of the doctors at the quarterly ALS clinic suggested that because my symptoms continued to be stable or even decreasing that I should come a day early at the next clinic to be retested.

Thursday we drove into Houston where I had the ALS tests rerun. At the end, the doctor who oversaw the testing said that my readings were normal and since the twitching had practically stopped, he was not surprised. Without going nuts, we waited till clinic the next day. When we got in to see Dr. Appel, he confirmed our understanding of the report. The ALS was gone. We did a lot of hugging and crying with the clinic staff and some of the patients. Dr. Appel wants to see me again in six months—unless something unforeseen develops. Then afterward, once a year. How do I feel? 1. <u>Thankful</u>. I don't know if this is a direct miracle from God or not, but I am thankful. And I am thankful to God. His goodness is true whether healing comes or not, but this is good. Thank You, Lord. 2. <u>Sad</u>. Too many good people are still trapped by ALS. It is a truly horrible disease. I pray for those few we befriended that God would bless them. And I pray for a cure. 3. <u>Confused</u>. Why me? In that confusion, I will speak judiciously in ways that I hope will not cause others to become bitter that I was 'healed', and their loved ones were not. 4. <u>Happy</u>. Being LaMon, I will never be worry free, but I am happy that I may have many years of ministry and life here. 7-2-11

From Psalm 22, 'My descendants shall serve Him.' I am thankful that Jason and Kari are serving God. I pray that their children will grow up to do the same. Lord, watch over Caitlyn, Jordan, Nico, Alex and Bella. Draw them to Yourself. 10-4-11

Lord Jesus I pray for Caitlyn, Jordan, Nico, Alex and Bella. Enliven their hearts and minds with the reality of your Presence. May they grow up to be young people and adults who love You and their neighbors. May they grow up trusting in You. 12-22-11

After our Trinity Group in March of 2012, I noted two important things in my journal. We had decided to do a book about some of our favorite prayers with commentary. It was published two years later as *Encountering God in the Prayers of Others*. The second was an idea I found helpful and which I shared from time to time in teaching and sermons. A person who had some very difficult times was asked how he could keep from being disappointed with God. His response, "I learned not to confuse life with God." This corresponded with a line from Ecclesiastes that has resonated with me for years, "Time and chance happen to them all." 9:11

I believe it was in late 2011 that I read a book that would eventually change my life. I don't think that is saying too much. The book is *Haiku—the Sacred Art: A Spiritual Practice in Three Lines* by Margaret D. McGee. I began to write haiku and would eventually use it as a means of lectio divina in Scripture reading. But all of that would come later. I mention it here as a seed that would bear wonderful fruit in my life.

My first haiku was written on a day I was parked in a restaurant lot waiting for Pat to get out of school:

A gentle breeze blows
Diesel fumes fouling the air . . .
Oblivious truck

I wrote the following on Easter morning: *After some office work, we headed for New Orleans. We ate lunch in Lafayette at Prejeans. It was a wonderful Cajun meal. . . . After taking some time to shop in an outlet mall, we got to our hotel in the late afternoon. It was old, but nice.*

. . .. We were blessed with a beautiful day Tuesday. We had breakfast at the Camilia Grill and then went to the French Quarter where we spent the day. We enjoyed beignets with café-o-lait at Café Du Monde and then had dinner at a little Mediterranean place down from the House of Blues. After breakfast at Le Madeleine's, we drove back to Bunkie. . . .. Then all hell (or hail) broke loose after midnight. We had the worse hailstorm any of us have ever experienced. Pat's car was totaled. We lost seven windows. The church probably lost thirty. 4-8-12

In June of 2012, we got emails and calls from some folks at First Baptist in Montezuma. Their pastor was retiring and already people were talking about the possibility of us returning there. Pat was excited about the possibility. My initial response was positive, but I realized that it might be somewhat depressing to go back after twelve years. Also, the uncertain future of church and town were similar to that of Bunkie. I did note that it would give me a chance to teach again at Mercer. I also noted that we had been looking forward to retiring and moving back to Albertville in 2013. I wrote that I felt like the old Jew in "Fiddler on the Roof".

Pat and I have been married for forty-four years. It has been a wonderful life and now looks like we could still have a stretch of years ahead—though no one ever knows. I thank You, Lord for our life together. I thank You for the love and joy that continues to be ours together. I could imagine a different life, but without my sweetheart, not a better one. Thank You, Lord. 8-2-12

In September, we went to Montezuma where I preached 'in view of a call'. The vote was unanimous for me to become their pastor—again.

My last sermon at Bunkie was a reworking of my last sermon at Montezuma twelve years ago. It is entitled "What I Believe". The structure is simple. I believe in Jesus; and because I believe in Jesus, I believe in forgiveness, fellowship, and the future.

Montezuma Pastor Again

We felt like returning was in some ways like going back home. While both of us grew up in Mt Calvary Baptist Church of Albertville, FBC Montezuma had had come to feel more like our home church. Whenever we were back in the States on home assignment, we would always go for a visit.

However, as we discovered, you can never go home again—things are always different. It is never exactly the same home. Three things became obvious. First, the congregation had changed. Many of the folks were still there from our first time. But some of the more moderate folks had grown old, moved away, or died. The first time there, I had lost a few members because of some of my sermons. This time it was even more difficult to proclaim the supremacy of the New Testament, the call of Jesus to love of enemy and non-violence, and the value of the Kingdom over against American nationalism. Second, since 9/11, FBC had followed most of America in becoming more nationalistic and supportive of American wars. Whereas I was able to move the American flag out of the sanctuary the first time there, I did not even consider it this time. Third, the economic situation, which was not great our first time there, had further deteriorated in the town of Montezuma.

Nevertheless, we enjoyed out time there. We reconnected with some of our friends. It was wonderful to be back with Howard as a music director who was always willing to follow my desires concerning music. He and Debbie remain good friends to this day. And we made new ones. The latter were Bonnie and Jule Windham who were there the first time, but for whatever reason, we were not the fast friends then that we became this time.

I also rejoiced in getting to baptize a good number of young people. I taught a young adult class for a while. I restarted the

Monday morning prayers with Communion. Attendance was better this time than the first time. As always, I felt good about my ministry to those who were sick and/or dying.

Beyond the church itself, I continued to write Sunday School lessons for Smyth & Helwys. And I returned to teaching on contract at Mercer University in Macon. I taught a survey of the Old Testament which I enjoyed more than though I might. I emphasized the changing understanding of God and religion that can be clearly traced, especially using the Hebrew order of books rather than the Christian order. I also taught a class on Eastern Religions. I enjoyed that class though I'm not sure I taught it as well as my predecessor did.

As I had done in Chiang Mai, so now I donated some of my books to a school. In this case, around 400 volumes went to McAfee's library. McAfee is the graduate religious studies program of Mercer University. It is in Atlanta.

Expressions of thanksgiving continued to bubble up:

My life is blessed. I give thanks for: my wonderful wife of almost 45 years, my son and daughter who are faithful to our Lord, my mom and dad who loved me to the end, my grandkids; each one special, my Trinity Group friends, my high school friends, my friends around the world—but especially in Chiang Mai, my friends in American Baptist life, my friends in Bunkie, my friends in Montezuma (Life can be measured by family and friends. If mine is measured that way, it is rich indeed), my ministry years (in India, Thailand, and America), my visits to Ireland, my relative prosperity, my health, my joy and peace, my religious experiences of prayer, Bible reading, Communion, meditation, silence, etc. My life is good. Praise God. 11-23-12

A few individual notes from 2013:

In February, I signed up for Medicare.

In March, I noted that I had begun writing haiku again on my readings in Psalms and the gospels.

In April, another member of our Trinity Group was found to have cancer. Paul Robertson told us it was incurable with a life-expectancy of 3 to 7 years. However, with experimental treatments and perhaps, our prayers, he was still going strong after 7 years.

The Trinity Group published *Encountering God in the Prayers of Others*. Several of us wrote about some of our favorite prayers. It was a great experience and resulted in probably our best collaborative book.

Pat suffered for months before the doctors finally determined that the problem was her gall bladder, which was removed.

I signed up to begin receiving social security benefits in August of 2013.

In November, I had a stint implanted in an artery that was 98-99% blocked. The doctor was surprised I had not already had a heart attack.

The highlight of the year was a wonderful retreat 3-18 through 3-23 at Mepkin Abbey with Catherine Powell as our spiritual director.

I found a book in the Mepkin library that moved my retreat experience to deeper levels. I eventually bought a copy for myself. It is "A Spiritual Psalter or Reflections on God excerpted by Bishop Theophan the Recluse from the Works of Our Holy Father Ephraim the Syrian.

I enjoyed the multiple services with the monks. We were encouraged to sit with them and join in the psalm prayers and singing. And although some of us were not Catholic, we were gladly allowed to receive Communion during daily Mass.

The highlight of the week was reading Song of Songs chapter 2. It enlightened everything else. In my journal I wrote several pages of notes from this deep and meaningful experience. I will record only some of the comments to give an idea of what was going on in my heart and mind.

Verse 1, 'I am a rose of Sharon, a lily of the valleys.' I thought what flower I would be, and it came to me—a little wildflower! I am fragile. I have beauty.

Verse 2, 'As a lily among brambles, so is my love among the maidens.' I am beautiful to God! Each of God's children is special. It is not that I am more beautiful than others, but that God seems for the moment to have eyes only for me.

Verse 3, 'With great delight I sat in his shadow, and his fruit was sweet to me.' I noted that it was important to taste what was in front of me rather than to desire other experiences.

Verse 4, 'He brought me to his banqueting house, and his intention toward me was love.' God intends to love me forever. And God intends that His love would create an answering love in me...

After finishing verse 4, I walked slowly toward the Refectory pausing and taking note of my wildflowers and other plants. I got to the dining hall too early so spent some time looking at the beauties of God's creation including a flock of birds frolicking in the big live oaks. It was then that I read this prayer by Ephraim. It so fit my mood and movement that I will set it down here:

> 'O God Lover of mankind! If Thy grace pours forth upon the grass, the flowers and all earthly vegetation in its time, then the more so shalt Thou grant to Thy servant that which he requests of Thee.
>
> For the air becomes clear and the birds adorn their voices with varied melodies, singing glory to Thy great wisdom. All the earth is clothed with a raiment of many-colored flowers woven without human hands and is glad and celebrates the holy day.
>
> Water also my heart with the dew of Thy grace, O good Lover of mankind! Just as a sown field cannot sprout and nourish its plants without sufficient rainfall so my heart is incapable of producing things pleasing to Thee and of bearing the fruits of truth without Thy grace.

>   Lo, the rain nourishes the plants, and the trees are crowned with diverse flowers. May the dew of Thy grace also enlighten my mind and may it adorn my heart with the flowers of contrition, humility, love and patience.
>   May my prayer draw near to Thee, O Lord! Grant me Thy holy seed, that I might bring Thee a harvest of sheaves abundant in good fruits and say, "Glory to Him Who gave me this that I might bring it unto Him," and bow down to the Father and the Son and the Holy Spirit.'

I shared this with others and every time it brought tears to my eyes.

Back to the Song of Songs:

Verses 8b-9a, 'Look he comes, leaping upon the mountains, bouncing over the hills. My beloved is like a gazelle or a young stag.' It is hard to imagine God as an animal, but certainly gracefulness is not foreign to God's Being. Graceful is a perfect word in thinking about God, to me at least, because it combines beauty and kindness—even gentleness. Not fragile, but gentle. God, you define graceful. You are the source of all beauty, kindness, and goodness in the world. . . . There is nothing so sublime as a gentle touch from almighty God.

Verse 9b, 'Look, there he stands behind our wall, gazing in at the windows, looking through the lattice.' This is the gaze of love. . . . To God, even in my sin, I am beautiful. I have God's image within and as a Christian, I have the Spirit of Christ within. I may not always see myself that way. And others may see defects, but God sees what glory may be hidden within which will one day be revealed. . . .

From verse 12, 'The flowers appear on earth.' I have been enjoying the flowers and by coming out to Christ, I have blossomed. . . . No plant blossoms all the time. And I know that one day the blossoms will fall away, and I will again have to be renewed in Christ. Help me Lord to not forget about this lest I become satisfied to be a plant without a bloom. . . .

From verse 13, 'The fig tree puts forth fig.' To change the metaphor from a wildflower to a fruit bearing tree, what fruit can I bear. This week I think I might bear gentleness, love, and patience. In so far as love is for persons, it manifests itself as kindness. . . . Lord I pray that by your creative power and grace that you will help me to have a three-fold bloom of gentleness, kindness, and patience.

As I noted, it was a wonderful retreat for which I remain thankful until this day.

In April, we bought our townhouse in Birmingham. We moved stuff over a little at a time.

We did various work there in both 2014 and 2015. Pat dug a ditch along the side of our yard to help with drainage. Our back yard could become muddy and wet because of drainage from the surrounding hills. The ditch helped a lot. We also did a lot of trimming and cutting back in the woods between us and the Cahaba River and the hill on the southside of our property. We planted flowers and trees. I created a succulent bed. And we created a wildflower bed as well. One big project was expanding our wooden deck in back. We love sitting out there, enjoying the nature view.

We made two trips in 2014. In the Spring we went to Gatlinburg and enjoyed the wonderful spring wildflowers and blooming trees. In the Fall we drove up to Vermont with Howard and Debbie. The Fall foliage was gorgeous.

Of course, I continued to pastor the church preaching, teaching, visiting, baptizing, having weekly Communion, and praying. One highlight at the end of the year was a black woman from the north who began to visit our church. She was married a southern, who moved back home to our area. He came occasionally. She was quite regular both in Sunday School and in worship. She even sang in the choir. Unfortunately, something happened in early 2015 that caused her to stop coming. I tried on numerous occasions to talk with her but was never able to make contact. (We had had a wonderful visit in her home months earlier.) I assume she encountered racism among our congregation, but never heard anything specific.

In the Fall I had a Trinity Group meeting in which we discussed John Polkinghorne's *Belief in God in an Age of Science*. I wrote, *in general, I have no issue with science unless the scientist pushes atheism. I accept [the scientific consensus] concerning evolution, global warming, millions of years of the existence of the universe, etc. I am only nervous about a neuroscience that would remove the element of human free-will—or at least, severely limit it. If that were true, then Calvinism wins.* 11-8-14

And another thanksgiving affirmation:

For all that follows, I am thankful Lord: my parents who nurtured my faith in various ways; Pat who is my constant companion and love; Kari and Jason who have shown the image of Christ to their world; Patrick and Lori who love my children and us; Caitlyn, Jordan, Nico, Alex, and Bella who are blessings to us all; Jesus Christ who enables me to know God; the Holy Spirit who makes me spiritually alive; the Father who wants me to call him abba; the Trinity Group who challenge me intellectually and strengthen me with lasting friendship; my health and prosperity; the Church—broken, yet faithful; the revelation of God found throughout the world; color; music; birds; plants; autumn, spring, and winter; friends beyond the Trinity Group; McGilvary Seminary; International Ministries of ABC; First Baptist of Montezuma; mountains and lakes; animal life, including pets; leisure opportunities; the Scripture, especially Psalms and the Gospels; my education that introduced me to the mystics and spiritual exercises like journaling; and opportunities to teach. For this and much more, I thank You Lord. 11-17-14

It seems the older we get, the more medical problems we run into. So, in early March, I had surgery to repair a torn retina. It took several weeks to get to that point, but the surgery was successful, and I have had no problems since.

When I die, I hope people can say, 'He loved Jesus Christ.' Or at least, 'He tried to follow Jesus.' 3-15-15

I don't believe that God has to be cajoled into helping someone or blessing someone. So, unless I feel a specific burden that causes me to pray more intently, a one or two sentence request seems appropriate. 5-22-15

I went to see Dr. Inhulsen this morning about some burning in my buttocks. We had a laugh or two. He gave me a phrase he thought I might be able to work into a sermon; protalgia fugax, "a fleeting pain in the arse". 9-9-15 I loved Dr. Inhulsen. He was married to a Mennonite lady. He also employed to Mennonite ladies in his business. I don't know if he was a Mennonite or not. He was a very good pianist who occasionally filled in for our regular pianist—the sweet, wonderfully talented Patsy Newberry.

Before our final Sunday at Montezuma, we attended a cookout in our honor at Bonnie and Jule's. We had a great time with a fine group of friends. Were I to attempt to name them all, I would fail, so I won't even try! *We got some nice cards and a couple of gifts. Debbie pained a beautiful cross that she mounted. It will definitely find a place in my office. It reminds me of the colorful Greek Orthodox crosses. 9-22-15*

On our last Sunday in Montezuma as pastor and pastor's better half, the church gave us several gifts. One was a stained-glass window that hangs in my study. Another was several nights in a cabin in Gatlinburg. Montezuma will always be part of our family.

Beginning My Retirement Years

On October 1, 2015, we began our new life in Birmingham as three! Caitlyn took a year off from attending classes at Lee University to work and save money. She took some online classes and worked at Publix. We loved having her live with us.

Before giving a brief summary of those first five years, a quote or two from these first months in retirement.

Here in no particular order, is a list of what I love: Christ (God & Spirit), Pat, family, friends, golf, birds, nature, sunsets, music, books, chocolate, hamburgers and beer, Italian food and red wine, quiet moments, sports of baseball & football, the color orange, old Volkswagens, Holy Communion, Taize music, hymns, laughter, going to movies with family and friends, the Trinity Group, Thailand—especially the north--, American Baptists, Ireland, stained-glass, Celtic crosses, poetry, Gatlinburg, Jazz Fest, New Orleans, Vermont, mountains, Fall colors, Spring flowers, first snow falls, Korat cats, rainbows, museums, bookstores, coffee shops, the gospels and the Psalms, journaling, writing, wildflowers, orchids, other blooming plants, etc. Thank you Lord for all the loves of my life and for a life that can know such love. 10-15-15

I have mentioned that in retirement, writing haiku will become increasingly important as a spiritual discipline. One of the first I wrote in retirement:

I trust in God
So, in darkness and in doubt
Still, I wait on Him

Responding to a quote from Miguel de Unamuno, "Those who believe they believe in God, but without passion in the heart, without anguish of mind, without doubt, and even in times of despair, believe only in the idea of God, and not in God himself", I wrote, *to believe in God, living in the kind of world in which we live, is not always easy! To believe in the face of doubt and despair-*

causing tragedies is to truly believe. Perhaps only those who are passionate about God truly believe. And so, I say, as I have said before, I believe Lord; help my unbelief. 11-2-15

As we were looking for a place to retire, I had a few requirements for a house. Two were a working fireplace and a nature view. Our new home has both. We have enjoyed using the fireplace in the winter months. And the nature view around our place is wonderful year-round.

As I mentioned earlier, Pat and I cleared out some of the brush and trees in the surrounding area. We also planted some trees, bushes, and perennial flowers. Then every year we have lined our deck with pots of flowers, plants, and herbs. In addition to that we erected several bird feeders. So, I enjoy sitting on the deck, looking at the foliage around me and the birds feeding at the feeders. Bird songs and cicada melodies float through the air.

I preferred city life for several reasons. One was access to good health care—which becomes more and more important the older we get. With some medical issues arising from time to time, we have both been pleased with our doctors and the health care system in general. I continue to have my retinas and my heart checked once a year. I have had one surgery to resection a portion of my bowel to remove a mass, which was benign. This was discovered as I was being treated for bowel problems and having lost some 30 pounds in a matter of several months. But as I write this, I seem to be on the mend.

Additionally, I looked forward to restaurants, coffee shops, movies, and music concerts—all of which I have enjoyed almost since day one.

We were blessed because Pat was quickly able to find a job with a company called ProctorU which specializes in monitoring online exams. She has found new friends there and believes that it is a place where she can bear Christian witness in a way that is natural and sweet. One of her passions in her free time has been craft work—lately a lot of quilts for friends and family.

Moving to Birmingham, we wanted to take our time in finding a new church home. We visited two Disciples of Christ Churches (also call Christian Churches). We visited four Baptist churches which were progressive—all with Cooperative Baptist Churches affiliation. However, only two of them were going certainly to remain progressive when their current pastor left. Eventually we settled on Baptist Church of the Covenant in downtown Birmingham.

BCOC was founded in 1970 when a large group of members and the ministerial staff left First Baptist when they refused to accept a young black girl's request for membership. So, BCOC was, from the first, a progressive Baptist church. Years later, they were probably among the first, if not the first Baptist church in Alabama to call a woman pastor. Early in her ministry there she received death threats. However, she persevered and was the pastor when we joined. Sarah Shelton is one of the finest preachers I have had the privilege to hear. Almost every Sunday her sermons were meaningful, full of biblical truth, and delivered in a winsome way.

BCOC became a welcoming and affirming church. Today a significant portion of the membership is LGBTQ. The wonderful Sunday School class that I eventually joined is led by a married lesbian couple who are raising two children they have adopted. I did not join the class for that reason, but because it used member participation to choose 'secular' songs to listen to that connected to the sermon topic. Sunday School met after worship service, plus Sarah always emailed our class late in the week to let us know what the focus of her sermon would be on. Most Sundays were filled with good music and intense discussion.

One of our reasons for choosing BCOC was that we have three friends who are members. Fisher and Caroline Humphreys are members, as is a friend and missionary colleague from India, Gail Hill. I thought I might be away some Sundays preaching and wanted Pat to be sure to have a place where she could set down some roots. Already having friends there was a wonderful plus.

I did, in fact, have preaching opportunities. Over the next several years, I filled in at a Disciples' church near Tuscaloosa when their pastor was away. I also preached at a couple of Baptist churches—again when their pastors were out of town. The only longer-term ministry was as interim pastor at a Disciple's church in Jasper, Alabama. I always enjoyed Disciples' churches because they were similar to Baptist churches in theology and they had deacon-led Communion every Sunday.

Living in Birmingham has been a pleasure, but we have also enjoyed traveling in the last few years. We went to Tennessee several times. Caitlyn was in school at Lee University. We visited with her on occasion. For our 50th wedding anniversary we went to Chattanooga. We really enjoyed the beautiful Fall colors in the area. I was inspired to write a few haiku. Here is one:

> Creativity
> Awesome beauty of nature:
> God without equal

We also met up with Caitlyn and her boyfriend Juan for a day there. Other trips included graduation exercises for Caitlyn and then for Juan. But the highlight was attending their wedding at Lee. I had the privilege of sharing in the service including serving the new couple the Lord's Supper.

We have continued to visit Gatlinburg once a year or so. It is always a thrill to see the natural beauty of the Smoky

Mountains. We enjoy wonderful meals—especially breakfast every morning at a different restaurant. And then there is the Donut Friar—no trip is complete without at least one visit there.

Another trip we made was to Florida where we visited with old friends. Rick and Ellen Burnette who had been missionary colleagues and Gerald and Kathy Wright, old friends from seminary days. Gerald is also a member of the Trinity Group.

Our last big trip was to California to visit with Jason, Lori, Nico, Alex, and Bella. The highlight of our trip was all of us going to Yosemite National Park. We had a great time. All the hiking proved my heart was strong! The scenery was beautiful. And we loved seeing our three youngest grandkids.

> Yosemite Falls:
> magnificent in height
> falling out of the sky

> sinuous red limbs
> perfect for contemplation:
> manzanita shrub

The last haiku reminds me that I want to complete this memoir with a recounting of some of the spiritual elements in my life these last few years.

Two continuing activities have been important. One, the Trinity Group has been part of my life for over 30 years. We do a lot of theology but sharing about our lives always has a spiritual dimension. The other has been my opportunity to continue doing spiritual retreats with Catherine Powel. The last one was held at the Jesuit Center in Atlanta.

> opening slowly
> patience of water lilies:
> a lesson for life

> a butterfly bush
> has identity crisis:
> a hummingbird drinks

The last haiku is a reminder that humor and spirituality are not antithetical!

Writing has always been important to me. In retirement, I have continued occasionally to write Sunday School material for Smyth & Helwys. Additionally, I started writing a blog under the title Pathways to God. The internet site is https://spirituality159.wordpress.com. My blogs can be accessed by clicking the blog button in the upper right-hand corner. They are listed from latest to earliest.

The biggest project was the publication with Michael Crane of a book that I had been working on for years, beginning in Thailand where I taught church history. It is entitled, *A Brief History of Christianity in Asia: Beginnings, Endings, and Reflections*. I first became interested in Asian expressions of Christianity as a seminary student in 1970 where I wrote a paper on the misnamed Nestorian Church in Asia.

Wednesday mornings eventually became one the high points of the week. Very early, I was introduced to a retired couple, Shelley and Jim Douglas, who had led peace vigils and anti-death penalty demonstrations for many years—the last several in Birmingham. So, most Wednesday mornings for about an hour, I stand on a corner in the Southside section of Birmingham holding a sign with several other vigilers proclaiming the value of non-violence and peace. One of the signs I hold has the first line of this haiku:

> there are no smart bombs:
> innocents always get hurt
> war never births peace

My commitment to non-violence goes back to my high school years where I was enamored with Mahatmas Gandhi, though Jesus was my primary teacher.

> Christ's mountain sermon:
> a way of non-violence
> a way of blessing

Over a year ago, I finally found an early morning Communion service to fill my weekly need for this blessing. So, on Wednesday mornings, I go to St. Luke's Episcopal church where I join 5 or 6 other folks for a short service of Holy Communion at 6:30. The timing is perfect as it gives me the opportunity to visit a coffee shop before beginning my peace vigil at 7:30.

A final piece of my retired life relates to what I have mentioned several times—writing haiku. Baptist Church of the Covenant has two special times during the year in which they offer three-week classes on Sundays and on Wednesday nights. I was asked to teach two classes. The first one was How Reading the Gospels Changed My Life. In that class, I also introduced the participants to writing haiku as a way to focus on the daily gospel reading. Several people picked up on the practice and really found it helpful.

This led to another one of those three-week presentations where I taught on The Spiritual Practice of Haiku. Using McGee's book as an outline, I taught what haiku was, why it is important, and how it can be used to deepen our spiritual life by focusing on personal histories, nature, scripture, and our own going lives. The essence of what I sought to teach was summarized in this haiku which became the theme of our continuing class:

> value of haiku:
> learning to pay attention
> making connections

The response of those three weeks was so positive that I agreed with the group that we would begin a new Sunday School class—focused on haiku. Two of the participants were members of the Quasi-Quaker class. Because Sunday School space is so limited, we worked out a schedule where the Quaker class would meet 1st and 3rd Sundays and the haiku class would meet 2nd an 4th Sundays. I was pleased with this arrangement for two reasons. 1) If we had weekly intervals between classes, I thought we would have more haiku and the experiences behind them to share. 2) I could maintain connections with the Folks class which had been so important to me in those first years at BCOC. We are a small class, but it is meaningful for all who participate.

In addition, I was invited to share about the spiritual value of haiku at a retreat by the board members of The Anchorage—the organization that Catherine Powell started years ago to help plan and support her retreats and that of others who joined the organization.

Future plans include having a retreat in which I and a woman from the Quaker and Haiku classes will lead. She will focus on the value of silence and I on the value of haiku. We are excited about the possibilities for there are several people who are interested in both topics but are unable to attend the Sunday School classes because they have other responsibilities.

I hope eventually to produce a book or two focusing on my haiku. I have written at least two haiku for ever psalm. The first time through, I normally meditated on the basic meaning of the psalm encapsulating it in a haiku. The second time through, I used more of a *lectio divina* method where I focused on a word or phrase. This often led to memories that inspired haiku.

I have also written haiku regularly on the daily gospel readings. Some days, no inspiration comes, but more often than not I can discover a meaning in the text or a connection between the text and life that leads to a haiku.

I also wrote haiku as I read through the books of Song of Songs (or Solomon) Ecclesiastes and Hebrews.

In addition to that, I have written many haiku related to nature experiences and life experiences. It helps me to pay attention. I believe we too often go through our days without any intentional awareness of important realities around us and in us. So, I have written hundreds and hundreds of haiku. I don't imagine many of them are publishable, but that is okay. The purpose of haiku is personal. It has been a life enhancer for me.

Conclusion

I am writing this on October 13, 2020. When I sat down to write this afternoon, I thought about writing something about the difficulty of 2020, but in the end, I decided all I really wanted to say, I had already written.

So, now I just want to add how much I love my family. Pat, my sweet darling wife of 52 years. My children, Kari and Jason, and their spouses, Patrick and Lori. And especially right now, my grandchildren and great grandchild, Caitlyn (and hubby, Juan), Jordan, Nico, Alex, Bella, and Eleanor. Perhaps in the years to come more great grandchildren will be born, and I pray God's blessing on them as well. Thank you all for the happiness and joy that you have brought into my life. May you walk all your lives following the one who shows us the say, Jesus Christ.

My Three Favorite Sermons

"Who Do You Say I Am?"
Mark 8:27-30

Today I want to give a personal answer to a question that Jesus asked. It is found in Mark 8:29; "Who do you say that I am?"

An old professor of mine affirmed, more than once, "I am captivated by Jesus." I feel the same way.

Dietrich Bonhoeffer who died in a German prison camp was right when he affirmed that when the church stops talking about Jesus, it has nothing to say. By which, he meant nothing to say that others are not already saying in one way or another. It is our commitment to Jesus that makes us truly different from the world. This is our defining characteristic.

So, who do you say Jesus is?

Here are a few answers I've picked up over the years.

The great Russian author Dostoyevsky wrote, "There is in the world only one figure of absolute beauty: Christ."

The Lebanese poet Kahlil Gibran affirmed, "In my heart dwells Jesus of Galilee, the Man above men, the Poet who makes poets of us all."

Martin Luther, with his usual bluntness, thundered, "You might just as well pray to the devil if you have to have any God but Jesus."

And there are lots more, but I'll end with a last one by Hugo Maynell, an English theologian.

"Christ is the light without which his people are in darkness, the shepherd without which they stray, the bread without which they starve, [and] the life without which they die."

But this morning I am not here to tell you what others say about Christ, but what I say. This is a kind of personal testimony. The only caveat I would add is that in a 15-minute sermon, I can't tell you everything I believe about Jesus, but I want to affirm three biblical images of Christ.

First, I believe in the Cosmic Christ.

Speaking of Christ, Paul wrote in Colossians 1:16-17, "in him all things in heaven and on earth were created, things visible and invisible, whether thrones or dominions or rulers or powers—all things have been created through him and for him. He himself is before all things, and in him all things hold together."

In John 1:3-4 it is stated the "all things came into being through him, and without him not one thing came into being. What has come into being in him was life and the life was the light of all people."

To use a camera analogy, this is the wide-angle lens view of Christ. It is in fact the widest angle.

Christ as the Logos or Word, or Christ as the eternal Son is vitally connected to all of creation. All things came into being in him and through him and for him. And all things are held together by him.

I love nature for many reasons, but one is that I can experience the presence of Christ in her. Her beauty is the beauty of Christ. Her song is the melody of Christ. Her fertileness is the life of Christ.

The stars twinkle with the joy of Christ. The moon shines with the reflected glory of Christ. The sun's light is a blessing of Christ on our world.

We can hear a mighty roaring river. We can see a majestic soaring mountain. We can rejoice in a field of wildflowers. All of this points to Christ.

Of course, I'm not naïve about nature. She can be harsh and cruel. And this is, in part if not in whole, because of human sin. In Romans 8:22, Paul pictures all of creation groaning as she awaits her full redemption.

Nevertheless, this aspect of fallen nature in no way disallows the glory of Christ shining through for all who have eyes to see.

I believe in the Cosmic Christ who is over all and in all, because all things have their being in him and through him and for him.

Second, I believe in the **Lord** Jesus Christ. If the Cosmic Christ is best seen through the wide-angle lens, the **Lord** Jesus is best seen though the telescopic lens; that lens which allows you to see things far away.

In the first Gospel sermon recorded in the Book of Acts, Peter wraps up what he has to say with these words, "Therefore let the entire house of Israel know with certainty that God has made him both Lord and Messiah [Christ], this Jesus whom you crucified."

And the word "Lord" was probably on the lips of Paul more than any other title as he spoke of Jesus.

So, this image can be found throughout the New Testament, but perhaps it is most dramatically seen in the Book of Revelation. Listen to some verses out of chapter one.

In verse 5, Jesus Christ is called the ruler of the kings of the earth.

And then John continues, "To him who loves us and freed us from our sins by his blood and made us to be a kingdom of priests serving his God and Father, to him be glory and dominion forever and ever. Amen."

Later in chapter one John has an awesome vision of the exalted Christ. He wrote:

^{12}Then I turned to see whose voice it was that spoke to me, and on turning I saw seven golden lampstands, ^{13}and in the midst of the lampstands I saw one like the Son of Man, clothed with a long robe and with a golden sash across his chest. ^{14}His head and his hair were white as white wool, white as snow; his eyes were like a flame of fire, ^{15}his feet were like burnished bronze, refined as in a furnace, and his voice was like the sound of many waters. ^{16}In his right hand he held seven stars, and from his mouth came a sharp, two-edged sword, and his face was like the sun shining with full force. ^{17}When I saw him, I fell at his feet as though dead. But he placed his right hand on me, saying, "Do not be afraid; I am the first and the last, ^{18}and the living one. I was dead, and see, I am alive forever and ever; and I have the keys of Death and of Hades.

The Book of Revelation, as indeed the whole New Testament, affirms that history is moving somewhere.

It is not a series of endless cycles; it has a goal. And that goal is the Lord Jesus who is the first and the last.

Just as I had to acknowledge that the harshness of nature may cause us to doubt the presence of Christ there, so it is with history.

Whether we are talking about world history or our national history or our personal stories, terrible things happen. There is war and disease. There is death in many, many forms. But I consistently refuse to believe that God is the cause of these things. As the writer of Ecclesiastes affirms in 9:11-12, "I saw that under the sun the race is not to the swift, nor the battle to the strong, nor bread to the wise, nor riches to the intelligent, nor favor to the skillful; but **time and chance** happen to them all. For no one can anticipate the time of disaster. Like fish taken in a cruel net, and like birds caught in a snare, so mortals are snared at a time of calamity, when it suddenly falls upon them." Yes, time and chance happen to us all.

So, when I say that Jesus is the Lord of history, I do not mean that everything that happens happens because of his express will or his passive will. Time and chance are realities in our fallen world.

But the world's hope is that Jesus **is** Lord. In the end, his will shall be done. This movement was set on its invincible way by his death and resurrection. Nothing can stop the fulfillment of his purpose to create a community of people who love God as they are loved by God and who love one another. Nothing can stop the creation of this eternal community of love. Nothing—not the ignorance of humankind, not the wiles of Satan, not the evil that stalks the world, nothing. Jesus Christ is **Lord**—the first and the last, the beginning and the glorious end.

We have used the wide-angel lens to see the Cosmic Christ overall and in all.

We have used the telescopic lens to see the Lord Jesus as the end of all history surrounded by a community of love—a community of his own making.

Now we have the close-up. I take just a picture of his face and I see there the face of my friend. In John 15:15, Jesus says, "I do not call you servants any longer, because the servant does not know what the master is doing; but I have called you friends, because I have made known to you everything that I have heard from my father."

Yes, as incredulous as it seems, the Cosmic Christ, the Lord of History is also my Friend. He walks with me. He guides me. He supports me. He never leaves me. And whenever I need it, he gently corrects me. Now, I certainly don't deserve his friendship, but as with any good friend, his presence makes me a better person. There is a friend who sticks closer than a brother—and his name is Jesus.

I close with parts of a poem by Scott Cairns:

And when, Lord Jesus, I chance to glimpse
     Your Holy Face it sets me once again
upon the way, both my Path and my sole Beckoning.
. . . .
In this way Your Face becomes my home,
     the radiance of my days, my realm
and sunlit land, where—all my life—
     I shall raise a murmur, uttering Your praise. . ..
Your visage bearing this immortal grace
     is like most holy myrrh to me. It is me
music and my instrument, my rest
     and resting place, my all and everything—Your Face.
Therefore, my sole desire is Your Face, and so
     I wish nothing more than this: that as I
contemplate Your Holy Mystery, I grow
     more fully to resemble you. O Jesus, press
upon me now some lasting trace
     of Your sweet, humble, ever-patient Face.

"How Thanksgiving Rescued Me"
Philippians 4:4-7

When I was in college, I read a devotional about a missionary in China. He had been imprisoned during the Communist takeover of that country. I don't know how long he was in prison, but he talked about how a particular passage of scripture helped him get through those dark days. It was Philippians 4:4-7.

What struck me in that story was the power of thanksgiving. And it changed my prayer life. Even today, almost all of my prayers begin with specific affirmations of thanksgiving.

Now I want to share two personal stories with you. This first one, some of you may remember from my ministry here earlier.

This first story took place in India in the early 80s. After we had been there over a year, Pat began to have some health problems. Eventually she had surgery at our mission hospital in Bangalore, India. Unfortunately, her symptoms quickly returned and the doctors there were at a loss as to what to do.

So, the decision was made for Pat to return to the States for more treatment. Because of visa complications and the uncertainty of how soon she might be able to come back, our two children and I stayed in India while Pat flew back to Alabama.

We were apart for eight weeks. It seemed like forever. Communication between India and America in the early 80s was very erratic. Making phone calls was next to impossible and letters could take forever. What little information I received in the first week or two was not encouraging. They were having trouble isolating the problem.

I became very depressed. I was in my 30s and it was the darkest time I had ever experienced. I was still teaching classes at the Christian college and I continued to care for our children. But

I had no joy, no peace. My prayer life had deteriorated to the point where all I did was beg God to heal my wife. I was afraid I might never see her alive again. Fear had become my reality.

Fortunately, years earlier, I had established a habit of morning devotions during which I would read scripture and write in my journal. In spite of my emotional state, I continued with that pattern. I had been reading through Philippians and one morning, I read again Philippians 4:4-7.

And it was like a light switch was flipped on. In my dread and fear, I had forgotten about praying with thanksgiving. So, right then I began to pray thanking God for his many blessings.

I thanked God for the wonderful years Pat, and I had had together. I thanked God for our children. I thanked God for the opportunity to serve in India. I thanked God on and on and on.

Then exactly what Paul promised happened. The peace of God that passes all understanding filled my heart. That phrase became more than words on a page. The peace I had was in some ways incomprehensible, which is what "surpasses all understanding" means. It was incomprehensible because I still did not know if I would ever see Pat alive again, or if I did what our future might hold. Nevertheless, I had peace.

Now that does not mean I was no longer concerned or that I quit praying for God to heal my wife.

I was still concerned, and I still prayed. But the almost paralyzing fear never returned. The peace of God remained.

The story ended with the kids and me returning to America where we were reunited with Pat. After a year, we were able to go back to the mission field without any further complications. I am so very thankful it turned out that way, but I believe that had it not, God's peace would still have guarded my heart and mind.

Now fast forward over 25 years.

It is 2009. Pat and I had made that hard decision to stay in the States. We had been missionaries with American Baptists in northern Thailand for 9 wonderful years.

In March of that year, I decided to see a neurologist. I had been having some pains in my legs and hips. I assumed it was a pinched nerve—which I had experienced in the past.

When I met the doctor for the first time, she ran some tests in the office and told me I might have Lou Gehrig's disease. I asked if Pat could join us so she could explain this to both of us. She agreed, so Pat was called into the office.

When the doctor told Pat what she had told me, I remember Pat asking, how ALS might be similar to certain muscular diseases. The doctor said it was similar, but that ALS usually progressed much faster. Three to five years was the normal life span for a person with Lou Gehrig's disease.

Although, the diagnosis of ALS was not definitely confirmed until January of 2010, in those first few weeks after the preliminary diagnosis was given in that March of 2009, I was a mess.

What little I allowed myself to read about the disease shook me to my core. I couldn't sleep. I wasn't hungry. I was so depressed that I quit buying books or music CDs! For those who know me, they will understand how drastically my life had changed. I was seriously depressed. It was so dark that momentary thoughts of eventual suicide floated around in my conscious mind. Now there was never any danger of following through on those thoughts, but it gives you an idea of how sinister those days felt.

I am sure there were several things that brought me back out of that darkness: the love of Pat and the grace of God being the two most important factors. But I also did something that helped.

I began making a Thanksgiving List. It is a chronological list going back to my childhood in which I have recorded remembered experiences for which I am thankful. Some were of great significance; others were less so. Many included persons who had blessed my life. For everything on my list, I was thankful.

I continue to work on that list, going back over it, remembering other happenings, and updating from time to time. Today, it probably numbers over 300 experiences. And if my memory were any better, it might be 1000.

Once again in a period of darkness, thanksgiving opened the window of my soul to the light of God's goodness and grace.

One of the lessons from my life that I hope to leave with the world is the happiness of thanksgiving. This is, I believe, one of the deep hungers of our world.

My prayer for you is that you will not wait until darkness comes before you remember to be thankful.

I shared this last story of ALS and thanksgiving several times as I pastored in Louisiana. Eventually I was able to add an update. We had had a year and a half of quarterly trips to an ALS clinic in Houston. From the beginning I had several symptoms—twitching of muscles in my legs, weakness in my hands, and loss of muscle mass.

But by June of 2011, the progress of the disease seemed to have stopped. They reran the tests, and the ALS was gone. I do not believe the original tests at the cline were wrong. The same experienced technician used the same instruments but came up with wonderful new results: there were no more signs of ALS.

The specialist in Houston had personally known of two other cases where this had happened: one of his own patients and the other, a doctor in Texas. It is extremely rare, but it does occasionally happen. And what he promised came to pass, e.g., my muscle mass and tone returned, and the ALS has not recurred. He said it would not.

It almost goes without saying that I am thankful! But I trust that even had I not been healed; I would still have had reasons to be thankful—everyday. And I fully believe that you do as well.

There is a cartoon of Pooh and Piglet walking through the snow:

>Pooh, "What day is it?"

>Piglet, "It's today."

>Pooh, "My favorite day."

If you are thankful, it can be your favorite day as well.

"Christian Forgiveness"
Colossians 3:12-17

Christianity can be called the religion of forgiveness. Humanity sinned against God and one another. Our relationship with God was broken. In Christ, God forgave the sin of the world. This is the Good News we proclaim.

But today, I want to talk primarily about Christian forgiveness: how we forgive others.

I was a missionary in India where I taught in a seminary in south India. During the summer months we had a 'Summer School of Evangelism'. People came from many places representing many vocations.

During that week, I preached a sermon on Christian forgiveness. The next morning one of the students who was a doctor had decided to leave early. He told me that he was returning to the hospital, but first he wanted to visit his father. He had not seen him for many years. He thought he could not forgive his father for doing wrong to him. Now he knew that he could. Needless to say, I was excited and hopeful for him.

Here is the essence of what he heard me preach. Forgiveness is important for at least three reasons.

1. People who do not forgive become more bitter. Bitterness is the fruit that grows in the soil of unforgiveness.

2. According to Jesus in Matthew 6:14-15, people who do not forgive are not forgiven. I don't know exactly what that means, but it sounds serious to me.

3. Forgiving fellow Christians makes God's family one.

That is one of the issues Paul is dealing with in today's passage. Learning how to forgive is similar to learning a skill. How do we learn a skill? We study with someone who knows, e.g. a cook, a guitar player.

Who can teach us how to forgive? Who is the master forgiver? GOD. We see God in Christ forgiving the world from the cross.

In verse 13, Paul wrote, "Bear with one another and, if anyone has a complaint against another, forgive each other; just as the Lord has forgiven you, so you also must forgive."

Paul says that we must forgive others like Jesus forgave us. Before describing that, I want to clear away some misunderstandings.

Some people believe that forgiveness is primarily a feeling like love. Therefore, if we don't feel loving or kind to a person, we can't forgive that person.

Did God love us before the cross? Of course, He did. If a feeling of love were the primary need for forgiveness, the cross would be unnecessary.

I am thankful that forgiveness is not a feeling. I can't always control my feelings. I am thankful that I can forgive a person without liking him or her. Forgiveness is not a feeling.

There is a second misunderstanding about forgiveness. Some people say that in order to forgive, we must forget.

What is $2 + 2$? 4. Now I want everyone to forget that $2 + 2$ equals 4. Could you do that? No. We cannot will ourselves forget anything. So, I am thankful that forgiveness is not forgetting.

On the cross, Jesus was bearing our sins, nor forgetting them.

So, what is forgiveness? Forgiveness is acceptance. This forgiveness has two sides.

First, we must accept the wrong done to us without seeking revenge. In The Shack God says to Mack, "Forgiveness is not about forgetting; it's about letting go of another person's throat."

Christ did not seek revenge. He could have called on a legion of angels. Instead, Jesus prayed for those who crucified him.

And that brings us to the second step.

We must accept the responsibility to help the one who has wronged us.

On the cross, Jesus was helping those who had sinned against him. Jesus was helping us. On the cross, he was preparing the way of salvation.

Forgiving another person means that we have decided to help him/her. When that person has need, we will try to help. But we don't have to wait on a crisis in that person's life. We can pray for the person. That is something we can do immediately. Pray that God will bless that person. In doing so, we imitate Jesus.

When we pray for God to bless a person with peace and love and salvation, we are forgiving the person who has wronged us.

In the Sermon on the Mount, Jesus is clear about how his disciples can respond properly to their enemies. He said, "Pray for those who persecute you." (Matt.5:44b)

In Summary:

Forgiveness is not tied to our emotions.

Forgiveness does not require forgetting.

Forgiveness is the decision to accept two things:

Accept the pain without seeking to hurt the pain-giver.

Accept the responsibility to help him.

Conclusion

About 30 years ago, a woman was teaching in a children's school. One day a man broke into the room. He forced everyone to watch while he molested one of the boys. That boy was the teacher's son. Later the police caught the man and put him in jail.

Do you think, she could forgive that man? For years, she thought she couldn't. She could not love him emotionally. She could not forget what she has seen with her own eyes.

However, one day she understood what forgiveness really was. That day she prayed for that man. And in praying for him, she forgave him. Eventually, the heaviness of her heart disappeared and she had peace.

Many years ago, I preached on forgiveness. Afterwards, one of them members said, "Brother LaMon you make forgiveness sound too easy."

I knew what she meant. Years earlier, her husband had been killed in a bar. She blamed the bar owner and carried this bitterness around in her heart. She did not want forgiveness to be easy. She wanted it to be so hard that she could be excused for not doing it.

I don't know what your situation is. But I have good news for you.

By dying on the cross, Jesus has forgiven all of our sins. And now we can forgive others.

If someone has hurt you, sinned against you, you can forgive them today. You can decide not to seek to hurt that person. You can pray God's blessing for that person.

Paul says, "Forgive . . . as the Lord has forgiven you."

www.ingramcontent.com/pod-product-compliance
Lightning Source LLC
Chambersburg PA
CBHW072020110526
44592CB00012B/1382